Terrorism

Look for these and other books in the Lucent Overview series:

Abortion
Acid Rain
Adoption
AIDS
Bigotry
The Brain
Cancer
Catastrophe in Southern Asia:
  The Tsunami of 2004
Chemical Dependency
Censorship
Cities
Civil Liberties
Cloning
Cults
The Death Penalty
Democracy
Divorce
DNA on Trial
Drug Abuse
Drugs and Sports
Drug Trafficking
Eating Disorders
Endangered Species
Epidemics
Environmental Groups
Espionage
Ethnic Violence
Euthanasia
Family Violence
Gambling
Gangs
Gay Rights
Global Resources

Gun Control
Hazardous Waste
Health Care
Homeless Children
Human Rights
Illegal Immigration
The Internet
Juvenile Crime
Legalizing Drugs
Mental Illness
Militias
Money
Multicultural America
Obesity
Oil Spills
The Palestinian-Israeli Accord
Paranormal Phenomena
Police Brutality
Population
Poverty
The Rebuilding of Bosnia
Saving the American Wilderness
Schools
Sexual Harassment
Sports in America
Suicide
Tattoos and Body Piercing
Terrorism
The U.S. Congress
The U.S. Presidency
Violence in the Media
Violence Against Women
Women's Rights
Zoos

Terrorism

by Diane Yancey

LUCENT Overview Series

LUCENT BOOKS

An imprint of Thomson Gale, a part of The Thomson Corporation

Detroit • New York • San Francisco • San Diego • New Haven, Conn. • Waterville, Maine • London • Munich

LIBRARY OF CONGRESS CATALOGING-IN-PUBLICATION DATA

Yancey, Diane.
  Terrorism / by Diane Yancey.
    p. cm. — (Overview)
  Includes bibliographical references and index.
    ISBN 1-59018-194-8 (hard cover : alk. paper) 1. Terrorism—Juvenile literature.
  I. Title. II. Series: Lucent overview series
  HV6431.Y355 2005
  303.6'25—dc22

                                                            2005016240

Printed in the United States of America

Contents

Introduction

What Is Terrorism?

TERRORISM IS A word that is on everyone's mind in the twenty-first century. The news regularly reports such terrorist acts as a subway bombing in Moscow, Russia; an attack on a commuter train in Madrid, Spain; the bombing of the British consulate in Istanbul, Turkey; and the bombing of the Australian embassy in Jakarta, Indonesia. World leaders, including President George W. Bush, President Pervez Musharraf of Pakistan, Prime Minister Tony Blair of Britain, and President Vladimir Putin of Russia, work to free the world from terrorism's grip. Ordinary people willingly give up some of their civil and personal liberties in order to help in any way they can.

Most people throughout the world would like to see terrorism eliminated. But as they try to come together to solve the problem, they discover that they do not all agree on just what terrorism is or who terrorists are. For instance, while Westerners see al Qaeda as a terrorist organization, some Middle Easterners see it as a group determined to cleanse Muslim societies of Western corruption. While many view the late Yasir Arafat as a terrorist who promoted violence, Palestinians grieve his death and remember him as a great leader who spent his life battling Israeli aggression. According to the UN Office on Crime and Drugs, "The question of a definition of terrorism has haunted the debate among states [countries] for decades. . . . Cynics have often commented that one state's 'terrorist' is another state's 'freedom fighter.'"[1]

Terrorists or Freedom Fighters?

Although there is debate over exactly what terrorism is, almost everyone agrees that a few common threads run through terrorist acts. First, they are violent. Next, they are intended to bring about change. Finally, their targets are usually unsuspecting civilians.

Some acts that are similar to terrorism are not classed as such. For instance, acts carried out by governments during a war—such as the dropping of atomic bombs on the Japanese cities of Hiroshima and Nagasaki during World War II—are not defined as terrorism. Guerrilla warfare, civil war, and open military aggression by an armed group are not generally considered terrorism because the participants tend to form large, heavily armed organizations and control territorial zones, while terrorists generally do not. Civil disobedience and retaliation against aggression are not considered terrorism if participants have no other means of making their voices heard.

Although Palestine Liberation Organization chairman Yasir Arafat was widely considered a terrorist, most Palestinians view him as a hero.

The difficulty in coming up with a general definition of terrorism usually arises when questions of motivation are added to the mix. When a cause is all-important and difficult to achieve and those who want it are frustrated and angry, they sometimes come to believe they have the moral right to use violence. People who agree with them, who think they are operating with the right motives, will not call them terrorists. Rather, they will see them as "God's warriors," "freedom fighters," or some other affirmative term.

Those who are attacked, on the other hand, see the picture from a different perspective. If they believe these so-called freedom fighters have not tried hard enough to make changes using peaceful means, they will see their motives as flawed. If what the attackers want runs counter to the common good, or if they ignore the wishes of the majority when they push for change, then they will not be seen as a positive force. Taking that into account, a decision to use violence might put these fighters into a class of criminals rather than heroes.

Rebel Chechen fighters such as these have been labeled terrorists by the Russian government.

It is often easier for those who are being attacked to say definitively that they are the victims of terrorism than it is for outsiders to decide whether or not a group is terrorist. Part of this is because outsiders are more objective: They are not being attacked and are thus less angry. Viewed objectively, issues can be so complex that definitive judgments are almost impossible to make. To avoid having to make such judgments, nations that are not directly involved often choose to remain neutral. In the conflict over Chechnya, for instance, the United States, Britain, and other world governments have neither recognized the Chechen government in its quest for independence from Russia nor designated the Chechens as a terrorist group. The Chechens see themselves as freedom fighters, while the acts they carry out are classed as terrorist attacks by the Russian government.

A Working Definition

Despite the fact that terrorism is a controversial subject, groups ranging from the Muslim World League, founded in 1962 to promote Muslim unity, to the United Nations have an official definition of terrorism on their books. Most definitions differ slightly, but are essentially the same. Terrorism is violence carried out by an individual or group in order to inspire fear and intimidation. It often has a political purpose—regime change, policy change, and so on—but the motivation can be religious, ideological, or political. It is not carried out by an army or government agent, although it may be sponsored by a government. It can be international, involving the territory or citizens of more than one country, or domestic, involving groups or individuals who are based within a country and whose activities are not directed by foreigners.

Even with a lack of agreement about terrorism, a number of countries, including the United States, have classed certain groups operating throughout the world as terrorist groups, and have learned as much as they can about the workings of these groups. Some of these groups operate in limited regions or on a small scale. Others are global, well funded, and adept at recruiting new members.

Specific steps to combat terrorism—from cutting off funds to going to war—have been taken by governments opposed to terrorism. At the same time, plans for the future are also being made, because terrorism is likely to change as the world moves further into the twenty-first century. As George W. Bush stated in February 2003:

> We must prepare our nation against the dangers of a new era. The grave threat from nuclear, biological and chemical weapons has not gone away with the Cold War. It has evolved into many separate threats, some of them harder to see and harder to answer. And the adversaries seeking these tools of terror are less predictable, more diverse. With advanced technology, we must confront the threats that come on a missile. With shared intelligence and enforcement, we must confront the threats that come in a shipping container or in a suitcase. We have no higher priority than the defense of our people against terrorist attack.[2]

1

The Scope of Terrorism

ALTHOUGH TRAUMATIC AND unsettling, terrorism is not a new phenomenon. In fact, the scope of terrorism is broad, stretching back through the centuries, weaving its way through history, and involving a variety of people and ideologies.

One of the earliest known instances of terrorism dates back to first-century Palestine (present-day Israel), when Jewish extremists called Zealots carried daggers under their cloaks and publicly stabbed any person committing what they judged to be a sacrilegious act (an act disrespectful to God). Ten centuries later, the Assassins, a secret group of fanatical Muslims who believed it was their religious duty to harass and murder those who deviated from strict Muslim law, also operated in the Middle East.

In the twentieth century, terrorist events included the July 1968 hijacking of a commercial airliner by the Popular Front for the Liberation of Palestine and the 1972 attack by Palestinians on eleven Israelis at the Olympic Games in Munich, Germany. The incidents demonstrated that terrorists had turned to mass murder as a means to achieve their ends, and highlighted the level of tension that has historically existed over disputed territory in Palestine and Israel.

Terrorists gained more attention in the 1980s as they began striking more often and taking more lives. Attacks such as the 1985 bombing of an Air India jet off the coast of Ireland (allegedly carried out by Sikh terrorists who wanted to

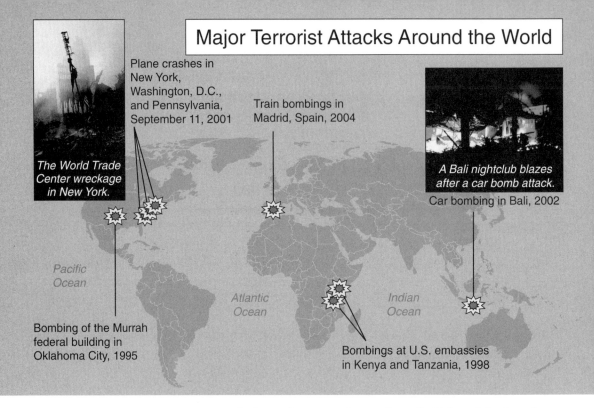

Major Terrorist Attacks Around the World

The World Trade Center wreckage in New York.

Plane crashes in New York, Washington, D.C., and Pennsylvania, September 11, 2001

Train bombings in Madrid, Spain, 2004

A Bali nightclub blazes after a car bomb attack.

Car bombing in Bali, 2002

Pacific Ocean

Atlantic Ocean

Indian Ocean

Bombing of the Murrah federal building in Oklahoma City, 1995

Bombings at U.S. embassies in Kenya and Tanzania, 1998

create an independent state in northern India) and the bombing of Pan Am flight 103 over Lockerbie, Scotland, in 1988 (sponsored by the government of Libya) killed more than 300 people each. The August 1998 bombings of the U.S. embassies in Kenya and Tanzania—before September 11, 2001, the largest attacks on major buildings—killed 224 people. They were carried out by al Qaeda operatives who resented the presence of Western troops stationed in Saudi Arabia.

The attacks on the World Trade Center and the Pentagon on September 11, 2001, were landmark events that claimed more than twenty-six hundred lives, including citizens from eighty countries. They also led Bush to declare war against terrorism. "Our war on terror begins with al Qaeda, but it does not end there," he stated in an address to the nation in September 2001. "It will not end until every terrorist group of global reach has been found, stopped and defeated."[3]

Motives for Terrorism

Americans and their allies in the war on terrorism live each day knowing that terrorists could strike again at any time. They are threatened by at least forty groups that operate in various locations around the globe. Although diverse, these groups all believe they are justified in using violence to achieve their ends. This is a fallacy, as author Carroll Payne notes: "Many terrorist groups believe they have exhausted all attempts at change through the normal political process and violence is the only recourse left available. However, very few . . . attempt to change society through the normal political process."[4]

Terrorists groups also fight for causes they believe are all-important or particularly meaningful. In general, there are five causes that motivate people to use violence: political ideology, racial/moral convictions, anarchism, religion, or nationalism. Of the five, religion (using violence to carry out supposedly divine commands) and nationalism (using violence to gain a separate independent nation/state) are by far the most common. Terrorists who are motivated by political ideology often want to overthrow capitalist governments and replace them with Socialist or Communist regimes. The Revolutionary Armed Forces of Colombia (FARC), established in 1964 by the Colombian Communist Party, is one of the few that are active at present. Those who have been active in the past include the Red Brigades in Italy and the Weather Underground in the United States.

Racial/Moral Convictions

Terrorists motivated by racial or moral convictions are often drawn from white supremacist groups such as the Ku Klux Klan, the Aryan Nations, and the neo-Nazis. They strike out violently against blacks and Jews and those who defend them. They also want to be as independent as possible; prefer small, local governments; and are opposed to the U.S. government, federal taxation and regulation, the United Nations, and other international organizations that get involved in people's lives. Most people from these groups who become terrorists are not well organized. They tend to be loners, formulating a one-man plan and then striking out alone against those they hate.

One of the most notorious men to be drawn from this category was Timothy McVeigh, who blew up the Alfred P.

Murrah Federal Building in Oklahoma City in 1995, killing 168 people and injuring hundreds more. McVeigh was angry about the federal government's treatment of white separatist Randy Weaver at Ruby Ridge, Idaho, in 1992, and its treatment of cult leader David Koresh and the Branch Davidians at Waco, Texas, in 1993. At Ruby Ridge, Weaver's wife and son were killed by federal snipers after a confrontation with Weaver over alleged illegal weapons sales. During the Waco incident, the Branch Davidian compound was burned to the ground, killing about eighty members of the cult. There was much debate over whether the fires were caused by cult members or government armored vehicles retrofitted with chemical weapons, and McVeigh was convinced that the legal outcome of the investigation was unfair. He thus felt that his terrorist act—which he timed to coincide with the two-year anniversary of the Waco fires—was entirely justified, as his response in 2001 shows:

> I waited two years from "Waco" for non-violent "checks and balances" built into our system to correct the abuse of power we were seeing in federal actions against citizens. The Executive; Legislative; and Judicial branches not only concluded that the government did nothing wrong . . . they actually gave awards and bonus pay to those agents involved, and conversely, jailed the survivors of the Waco inferno after the jury wanted them set free.[5]

Anarchism and Antiglobalization

Terrorists motivated by a desire for anarchy are similar to those who are motivated by racial/moral terrorism. The word *anarchy* here does not imply chaos or mob rule, but rather a stateless society with voluntary social harmony.

In past decades, anarchist terrorists sometimes carried out their goals by assassinating government leaders. From 1870 until about 1920, revolutionaries seeking to overthrow established governments launched waves of bombings and assassinated a series of heads of state. One victim was President William McKinley, killed in 1901 by a young Hungarian refugee influenced by anarchist sentiments.

As time passed, the anarchist movement changed. Twentieth-century anarchists put aside their determination to kill gov-

Timothy McVeigh was convicted of the 1995 bombing of the Murrah Federal Building in Oklahoma City.

ernment leaders and instead decided to bring about change by educating ordinary people, creating grassroots groups that would rise up and take action. Thus, anarchists became involved in labor, animal rights, ecological, and feminist movements. They protested cutting of old-growth forests, blocked destruction of the rain forest, and marched in support of women's rights.

In the 1990s they also became involved in protests against meetings of the World Trade Organization (an international organization based in Geneva, Switzerland, that monitors and enforces rules governing global trade) that took place in Washington, D.C., Seattle, and other locales. Anarchists are against government and big business, and thus strongly oppose such gatherings. Although most anarchists are nonviolent, these protests involved property damage. Author and ecologist Paul G. Hawken explains, "They . . . do believe that

Opponents of the World Trade Organization stage violent protests at the WTO meeting in Seattle in 1999.

property damage . . . is a legitimate form of protest, and that it is not violent unless it harms or causes pain to a person. For the [anarchists], breaking windows is intended to break the spells cast by corporate hegemony [authority], an attempt to shatter the smooth exterior facade that covers corporate crime and violence. That's what they did [in Seattle in 1999]."[6]

Religious-Motivated Terrorism

Most terror attacks that take place throughout the world today are motivated by religious ideology. Sometimes they are carried out by Christian or Jewish fundamentalists who believe God is calling them to take action against people who are disobeying his laws. More often, religiously motivated terror is carried out by militant Islamic fundamentalists, Muslims who believe that every verse in the Koran (the Islamic holy book) must be followed to the letter. They acknowledge no law but sharia—Muslim law—which is conservative and leads them to ignore human rights, reject people of different faiths, and scorn the liberal principles of modern society. They use extreme interpretations of passages and justify terrorism through sharia and jihad. They interpret jihad to be holy war against God's enemies, even though more moderate Muslims justify its use only when a Muslim homeland has been attacked.

Many people hold fundamentalist beliefs because they are poor, frustrated, and angry with the corrupt governments that rule over them. They find in their religion God's promise of a better life, both on earth and later in heaven, if they follow his commandments to the letter. Thus, they are highly motivated to please God, gain rewards, and punish the sinful. If they can bring about the establishment of Islamic governments, they also believe they are returning righteousness to the world as well.

Power and Prestige

Not all fundamentalist Muslims are poor and oppressed, however. Instead, some are angry that people of their faith have been treated as second class citizens by powerful Western countries such as the United States for many years. They resent past Western actions in the Middle East, such as the arbitrary cutting up of the region into the nations of Israel, Iraq, and Lebanon after World War II. They resent recent Western actions such as Operation Desert Storm in the 1990s and the Iraq war, both of which caused Western troops to be stationed on Saudi Arabian soil. (Saudi Arabia was the home of the prophet Muhammad, the birthplace of Islam, and is therefore the most sacred site to Muslims.) They are unhappy that Western culture and Western values have permeated Middle Eastern society. As foreign policy expert Thomas W. Lippman notes, "If you go to the most modern shopping mall in Saudi Arabia, it looks entirely American, except for the veiled women. If you go to the food court, there's a McDonald's, a Pizza Hut and a Burger King."[7] These Muslims embrace terrorism in the hopes of weakening Western power and Western influence in the world.

Some embrace terrorism with the goal of establishing a Pan-Islamic state. This could either be a large region with no

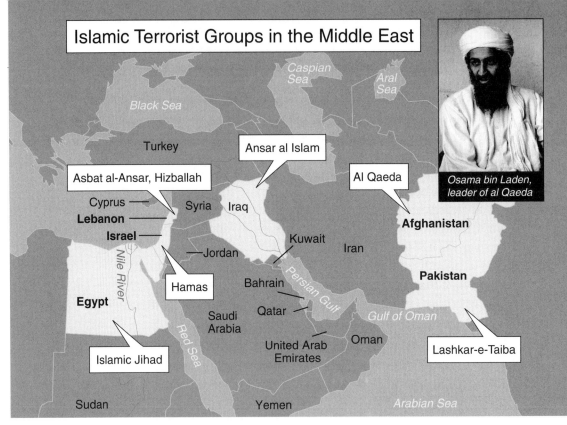

Islamic Terrorist Groups in the Middle East

Osama bin Laden, leader of al Qaeda

borders where Muslims would live under Muslim law, or it could be a situation in which all Muslim countries live in harmony together. In either case, once it is established, Muslims would cooperate within it to regain the power and prestige the Islamic empire enjoyed before the eighteenth century.

Many Islamic fundamentalist terrorist groups exist in the world today. The most well known is al Qaeda, led by Saudi multimillionaire Osama bin Laden. Founded in 1988, the organization is believed to have thousands of followers, along with supporters who are members of other terrorist groups who share its aims. These include Asbat al-Ansar in Lebanon, Islamic Jihad in Egypt, and Lashkar-e-Taiba in Pakistan. Journalist Jim Garamone writes, "[Al Qaeda] is a loose coalition of groups with a total of about 3,000 members. The network has a global reach, with cells in more than 30 countries—including the United States, as the events of Sept. 11 indicated."[8]

The Palestinian Cause

While al Qaeda fights to push the West out of Saudi Arabia, it joins other Islamic terrorist groups in a nationalist movement calling for the removal of the Jews from Israel and the establishment of the nation of Palestine there. These groups believe the land that comprises modern-day Israel was given to Muslims by God around the first century A.D. Jerusalem, the capital of Israel, contains the al-Aqsa Mosque and the nearby Dome of the Rock, a golden-domed structure that encloses the rock from which the Muslim prophet Muhammad is said to have ascended into heaven for a time. Al-Aqsa and the dome are two of the most sacred sites of Islam.

In order to regain land they believe is rightfully theirs, Palestinian nationalists are willing to use terrorist tactics to drive everyone else out. Bin Laden wrote in November 2002, "The creation of Israel is a crime which must be erased. Each and every person whose hands have become polluted in the contribution towards this crime must pay its price, and pay for it heavily."[9]

The number of groups dedicated to Palestinian nationalism is too large to detail. One of the biggest and most well known is the terrorist organization Hizballah, also known as the Party of God, which is based in southern Lebanon. It was formed in response to the Israeli invasion of that country in

Jerusalem is home to many holy sites such as the Wailing Wall (foreground), which is sacred to Jews, and the Dome of the Rock (right, background), sacred to Muslims.

1982. With a few hundred operatives and several thousand supporters, it has established cells in Europe, Africa, South America, North America, and Asia. Hizballah takes its ideological inspiration from the teachings of the late Ayatollah Khomeini, a radical Muslim who was the leader of Iran. Led by Lebanese fundamentalist Hassan Nasrallah, its members are dedicated not only to the elimination of Israel and the creation of Palestine, but also to the establishment of Islamic rule in Lebanon.

One of the most active terrorist organizations that combines Palestinian nationalism and religious fundamentalism is Hamas (Islamic Resistance Movement). Hamas was formed in 1987 and has an unknown number of members, although thousands support it. It operates out of Palestinian refugee camps in southern Lebanon, the West Bank, and Gaza, and has pledged to destroy Israel, establish an Islamist Palestinian state, and raise "the banner of Allah over every inch of Palestine."[10]

To Establish an Independent State

While many Islamic terrorists focus on Palestine, other terrorist groups want to gain independence from established governments in other parts of the world. For instance, Abu Sayyaf in the southern Philippines seeks to establish a separate Islamic state for the country's Muslim minority in western Mindanao and the Sulu Archipelago.

Chechen separatists, who have been fighting for their region's independence from Russia since 1994, are not classified as terrorists by the U.S. State Department, but experts note that those involved in the fighting have connections to international Islamic terrorists and use terrorist methods such as hostage taking, bombing, and using suicide bombers. In August 2004, for instance, two suicide bombers with links to both Chechnya and al Qaeda killed and injured more than sixty civilians in a Moscow subway station.

Faced with a group that has all the hallmarks of a terrorist organization, the Russian government has not hesitated to label the Chechens "terrorists." Vladimir Putin stated, "[The rebels] are not only linked with international terrorist organizations but have become an integral part of them, perhaps the most dangerous part. . . . Not a single government in the world will be pushed around by terrorists. Nor will Russia."[11]

Some three thousand miles south of Chechnya, the Liberation Tigers of Tamil Eelam (LTTE), who fight for an independent Tamil state in the northern and eastern provinces of Sri Lanka, are considered vicious terrorists by many of the world's leading nations. The Tamils, most of whom are Hindu, make up about 18 percent of the population in Sri Lanka, an island off the coast of India.

Founded in 1976, the LTTE is led by Velupillai Pirabakaran and is estimated to have eight thousand to ten thousand armed combatants, with a core of three thousand to six thousand trained fighters. Its activities against the government

The rebel group Liberation Tigers of Tamil Eelam (LTTE), known as the Tamil Tigers, is considered a terrorist organization by the Sri Lankan government.

have included two massive truck bombings and attacks on ships in Sri Lankan waters, plus attacks on civilians on mass transit, at Buddhist shrines, and in office buildings. The group argues that such violence is necessary in order to achieve the freedom its members crave. Pirabakaran stated in 1999, "Eelam is our homeland. . . . Our liberation war is essentially a war to liberate our lands and to establish our sovereignty: our right to rule in our homeland."[12]

"This Land Is Our Land"

Asia is not the only region where groups use violence to gain independence or reclaim their homeland. In northern Spain, the Basque Fatherland and Liberty group, *Euskadi ta Askatasuna* (ETA), turned to terrorism decades ago in hopes of breaking free and forming an independent state. The Basques are a linguistically and culturally distinct group that lives in the mountainous region straddling the border between Spain and France.

Formed in 1959, the ETA has been responsible for almost 850 deaths since the late 1960s. Its bloodiest year was 1980, in which 118 people were killed. Today, the group has about twenty members and several hundred supporters who target Spanish officials as well as civilians. In May 2005, they set off powerful car bombs in Madrid, injuring 52 people.

The Irish Republican Army (IRA), formed in the 1970s, has also killed hundreds in its quest to gain independence for Northern Ireland from the British. Although, in the words of the Irish poet Patrick Galvin, its members only want to know "that this land is our land . . . a green land without death,"[13] they gained a fierce reputation as they conducted bombing campaigns against various targets in Northern Ireland and Great Britain. These included senior British government officials, civilians, police, and British military. They also carried out assassinations, kidnappings, and beatings that took the lives of eighteen hundred people, including six hundred civilians.

After IRA bombs killed civilians attending a Remembrance Day ceremony and two children were killed in Warrington, England, in 1987, tens of thousands of people began

calling for an end to the IRA's violence. As a result, the organization gave up its campaign of terror in 2000. However, offshoot organizations—the Real IRA (RIRA) and the Continuity IRA (CIRA)—continue terrorist activities that include bombings, assassinations, kidnappings, and "punishment beatings" of those Irish who are loyal to England. In late 2004, RIRA used fifteen firebombs against shops and businesses in Belfast, the capital of Northern Ireland.

This June 1974 fire at Westminster Hall in London's House of Parliament was caused by an IRA bomb.

The Threat in Perspective

With so many terrorist groups in the world, and with reports of terrorism everywhere, the likelihood of an attack seems overwhelming at times. When the numbers are studied closely, however, the threat looks less alarming. Figures released by the U.S. government in mid-2004 show that the number of attacks worldwide has fallen since 2001. There were 208 acts of international terrorism in 2003, a slight increase from 198 in 2002. The number of those killed worldwide in 2003 totaled 625, with more than 3,500 persons wounded. In 2002 the numbers were 725 and 2,013. All in all, the numbers give a picture of stability that is somewhat reassuring.

Other comparisons put the threat into better perspective. For instance, the fewer than one thousand deaths worldwide that result from terrorism every year pale in comparison to the fifteen thousand murders that take place in the United States annually. They are an even smaller fraction of the forty thousand automobile deaths that occur there every year. As journalist and statistics expert Bart Kosko points out, "There will always be terrorists and legitimate efforts to catch and kill them. But meanwhile, the bigger statistical threat comes from the driver [in the car] next to you who is talking on the cellphone."[14]

2

The Logic and Tactics of Terrorism

TERRORIST VIOLENCE APPEARS to be random and senseless to the casual observer, but it is carried out with very definite goals in mind. The first is to frighten and overwhelm. As Australian attorney general Philip Ruddock noted in 2004, "The terrorists want to intimidate the general population. . . . They want us to be hesitant [and] conservative."[15] The second is to use that intimidation to push through a social or political plan.

This well-defined logic, then, governs the way terrorists go about choosing their targets, planning their timing, and determining their means of attack. Symbolism plays a large and important part in that decision making, as does publicity. According to the Terrorism Resource Center, "The terrorist needs to publicize his attack. If no one knows about it, it will not produce fear. The need for publicity often drives target selection; the greater the symbolic value of the target, the more publicity the attack brings to the terrorists and the more fear it generates."[16]

To Horrify and Manipulate

When terrorist attacks are fine-tuned, the resulting violence has a huge psychological impact on a large number of people, even though relatively few may be harmed by it. The events seem so bewildering, random, and evil that many cannot take them in. Regarding the September 11, 2001, attacks on the World Trade Center and the Pentagon, journalist and

U.S. Army major Mike Pelletier writes, "The effect of 9/11 on our society was profound. . . . Initially, there was great fear, as it seemed the terrorists were everywhere. This was followed by shock, as we desperately tried to understand the event."[17]

To maximize the shock and horror, terrorists often strike when everyone is preoccupied with other activities—particularly enjoyable ones, so the contrast will be great. For instance, in March 2002, ten people were killed and fifty were injured when the al-Aqsa Martyrs Brigade attacked a bar mitzvah (coming of age) celebration in a Jerusalem neighborhood. Also in Israel in October 2003, twenty-one people were killed and seventy-one injured while enjoying dinner at a beachfront restaurant in the town of Haifa on a Saturday afternoon.

An unexpected disaster is especially traumatic to victims and witnesses, so terrorists never forewarn of their attacks. The public is not alerted. The police are given no clues. In the case of simultaneous suicide bomb attacks on three London underground trains and a London bus on the morning of July 7, 2005, even counterterrorism officials who can gather intelligence by tapping suspects' phones, reading e-mails, and trading intelligence with other countries, were taken by surprise because no word of the planned strikes had leaked. The bombings killed at least fifty-five people, injured more than seven hundred, and stunned millions who had been involved in their everyday routines when the blasts brought the city to a standstill.

To Punish the Guilty

The fact that terrorists intentionally target and kill random civilians is a particularly disturbing aspect of their strategy. Premeditated killing is usually associated with war, capital punishment, or crime. Terrorists deliberately kill anyone who happens to be at the target location, which is almost impossible for most ordinary people to comprehend.

Many people are also disturbed by the notion that terrorists target women, children, and the elderly—people generally considered immune from attack. Terrorists, however,

Islamic terrorists were responsible for a series of deadly bombings in London in July 2005.

operate on a different standard. The simple fact that a person does not share the terrorist's beliefs makes him or her evil. For Osama bin Laden, for instance, the fact that a man is an American citizen or has paid U.S. income taxes is enough to make him guilty of complicity in his government's actions—and therefore deserving of death.

To Sway Public Opinion

After a terrorist strike, victims and witnesses feel shaken and extremely vulnerable. They feel like they could be hit again anywhere and at any time. The enemy thus appears looming, ominous, and extremely powerful. Having to think about dealing with such an enemy again in the future is often too stressful to bear. When faced with such a possibility, the public might react by pressuring their government to compromise in order to cut down on the risk of future attacks. Governments are often more than willing to agree to their wishes.

This is just the result terrorists hope to achieve. One of their primary goals is to intimidate and sway governments to effect political change. Such was the case in Spain in 2004. Spain was one of the few coalition countries that had troops fighting in Iraq, and in March of that year, terrorists affiliated with al Qaeda bombed a commuter train in Madrid, killing 191 passengers and injuring more than 1,500. In the days following the incident, the Spanish people reacted by voting out the old government and electing a new one that pulled Spanish troops out of Iraq. Their departure was a psychological victory for insurgents, including al Qaeda agents, who went on to increase the fury of their violence against the procoalition forces that remained in Iraq.

Nearly two hundred people were killed and more than fifteen hundred injured in the March 2004 terrorist attack on commuter trains in Madrid.

While al Qaeda achieved its ends in Spain in 2004, more often the intimidation tactic does not work. Just a few months later, when the Spanish government offered to hold talks with Basque terrorists following a May 2005 attack in Madrid, hundreds of thousands of Spaniards took to the streets in protest. "Many people have died at the hands of these assassins," said Maria del Carmen Fernandez, who lost her husband in a car bomb attack in Madrid in 1981. "We don't want to negotiate with the people that killed our loved ones."[18]

To Make a Symbolic Point

At the same time that terrorists try to intimidate and sway public opinion, they also choose targets that are in some way symbolic to themselves and to their enemies. Symbolic targets have great meaning to a great number of people. Thus, the destruction of just one symbolic target emphasizes the terrorists' power and inflicts great pain and sadness upon millions of people in one moment.

When taking symbolism into account, government buildings are the first to be considered. They are symbols of authority and leadership, so striking them—especially a nation's capitol building—demonstrates the vulnerability of the nation's leaders. Destroying military bases symbolizes the destruction of a nation's military might. On September 11, the World Trade Center was struck because it was a much-despised symbol of Western capitalism and materialism. Terrorist expert Robert T. Thetford notes, "The Twin Trade Towers were most likely chosen because of their representation, at least in the eyes of the terrorists, of . . . such American ideals as strength, achievement, financial stability, capitalism and even democracy itself."[19] There is further speculation that the 9/11 terrorists chose to fly on United and American airliners because these planes had names symbolic of America and the United States that the terrorists hated.

Not only places but also dates are considered worthy symbols by terrorists. In mid-December 1999 al Qaeda agent Ahmed Ressam was caught trying to smuggle explosives into the United States as part of a plot to bomb Los Angeles International Airport on December 31, 1999. This attack would have come during millennium celebrations, when the Western world was welcoming in a new century. If the attack had been successful, the terrorists, who believe God forbade the calculation of months and years using the West's Gregorian calendar, would have been able to demonstrate their power and superiority by disrupting the celebrations.

Many people believe Independence Day—the Fourth of July—is another natural date for terrorists to target. Not only is it a national holiday, it stands for all that Americans hold dear—democracy, freedom, family, and the flag. Any terrorist strike on the fourth would be seen as a symbolic strike at the heart of America itself. As one federal law enforcement official states: "The Fourth of July is about as symbolic as they come. To pretend that our national holiday wouldn't be an enormous propaganda target for al-Qaida is dishonest."[20]

Bombs: Weapons of Choice

The logic that terrorists like Ahmed Ressam use in formulating their attacks on the West is often difficult for ordinary people to understand. The tactics and weapons they use to carry out those attacks, however, are less complex.

Bombs have always been highly favored terrorist weapons—they are visible and highly destructive, and thus draw much public attention. Over the years, terrorist bombs have ranged from handheld devices to mail bombs, from almost undetectable amounts of plastic explosives hidden in shoes to delivery trucks full of chemicals and fertilizer. Bombs are frequently used because they can be set to go off at a future time, giving perpetrators time to get away.

Suicide bombs are weapons of choice because bombers are able to wait for the best time and place to detonate their weapon. Suicide bombers are individuals who strap explosives to their bodies, then go into a targeted area and detonate the bomb, killing themselves and everyone around them. Their act is not only effective, it is extremely dramatic and symbolic in that the death of the bomber emphasizes his sincerity and willingness to sacrifice everything to advance his cause.

The suicide bomb is also virtually a perfect weapon in that it is almost impossible to stop. The suicide bomber looks like everyone else. He or she hides the explosives in ordinary-looking articles that rarely raise suspicion. The first clue that the attack is about to take place is the explosion itself. Journalist Thomas Friedman observes, "When you have large numbers of people ready to commit suicide, and ready to do it by making themselves into human bombs, using the most normal instruments of daily life—an airplane, a car, a garage door opener, a cell phone, fertilizer, a tennis shoe —you create a weapon that is undeterrable, undetectable and inexhaustible."[21]

Hostage Taking

Kidnapping is another tactic that terrorists have used for decades and continue to use today. Hostages can be held for ransom, but they can also be held to make other points. Terrorist groups often send videos of Western hostages they have captured to Middle Eastern television stations. On the videos, which are sometimes aired for the public, the hostages are shown being abused and even killed. The pictures send vivid messages that the terrorists are ruthless and uncompromising. During the war in Iraq, the images caused some companies and national leaders to withdraw their people from Iraq for fear they would be hurt. International affairs expert Ibrahim al-Marashi observes, "Videos of kidnapped hostages have proved successful in forcing world leaders to withdraw troops from Iraq [and] preventing international firms from participating in reconstruction efforts. . . . Therefore, however repugnant is the footage, it constitutes a success for the insurgents in attracting world attention to their cause."[22]

One of the most high-profile abductions in recent times was the kidnapping of *Wall Street Journal* reporter Daniel Pearl in January 2002. Pearl was taken in Karachi, Pakistan, by members of Jaish-e-Muhammad, a militant Islamic group protesting Pakistan's cooperation with the United States in the Afghan War. He was held for several weeks, and then a videotape showing his murder was released to the press. The

Algerian Ahmed Ressam was arrested at the U.S.-Canadian border in December 1999 trying to smuggle explosives into the United States for a terrorist attack on Los Angeles International Airport.

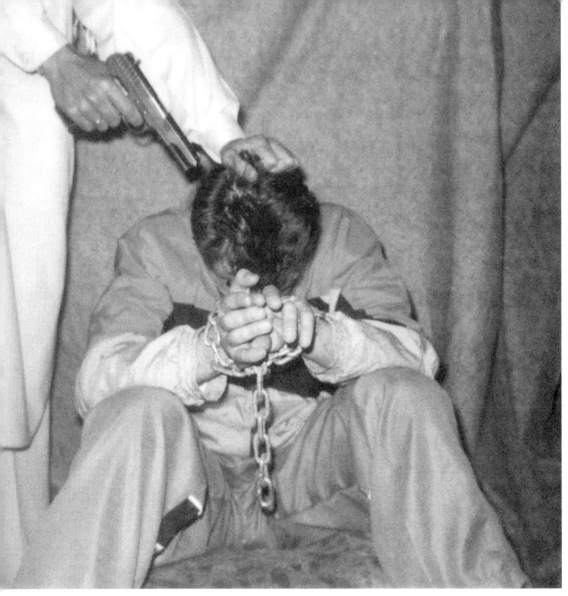

In 2002 American journalist Daniel Pearl was kidnapped and executed by Islamic terrorists in Pakistan.

terrorists made sure their purpose was clear when they emphasized on the tape: "We assure Americans that they shall never be safe on the Muslim Land of Pakistan. And if our demands are not met [the release of prisoners at Guantánamo Bay and the end of the U.S. presence in Pakistan, among others] this scene shall be repeated again and again."[23]

Kidnapping targets have included diplomats, businessmen, tourists, and missionaries as well as journalists. In what was perhaps one of the largest groups of hostages ever taken, Chechen rebels held more than seven hundred theatergoers captive in Moscow in 2002, demanding the withdrawal of Russian forces from Chechnya. Apparently the incident was designed to be a fight to the death, illustrating the desperation of the hostage takers. After a two-and-a-half-day siege, Russian government forces raided the theater, resulting in the deaths of the rebels and more than one hundred hostages. Journalist Olga Chernyak, one of the surviving hostages, remembers, "The terrorists, especially the women among them, told us frankly: 'We have come here to die, we all want to go to Allah, and you will be going with us.'"[24]

Weapons in the Sky

Passengers on commercial airliners are another favorite target of terrorist kidnappers. Trapped in their seats inside a thin metal shell, thousands of feet above the ground, and at the mercy of whoever is controlling the plane, they become helpless hostages that the hijackers can threaten to kill if officials on the ground do not give in to their demands. Airplane hijacking (also known as skyjacking) began in the late 1960s. Terrorists hijacked planes to Cuba or held passengers aboard planes for long periods of time with no food, water, or sanitary facilities. This was usually done as an attempt to force a government to grant concessions such as the release of fellow terrorists from prison.

One of the most famous skyjacking incidents was the June 1976 hijacking of an Air France plane by Palestinian and West German terrorists who demanded the release of fifty-three terrorists from various prisons in Europe. The hostages were flown to an airport in Entebbe, Uganda, where Israeli commandos carried out a daring rescue. The hijackers were killed, and three of the hostages died in the raid.

Hundreds of skyjackings took place between 1976 and 1996, although the annual rate of occurrence began declining around 1980. By the year 2000, skyjackings had become a relatively uncommon terrorist tactic. Then, on September 11, 2001, nineteen members of al Qaeda hijacked four passenger airliners from U.S. airports, piloting two of them into the World Trade Center in New York City, one of them into the Pentagon in Washington, D.C., and crashing one in a field in Pennsylvania. The idea that airliners could be used as suicide bombs stunned the world. Few had foreseen that terrorists would take something so ordinary as airplanes and turn them into weapons that quickly and easily killed thousands of people. The fact that they had struck on American soil was chilling, too. Terrorists seemed closer and more menacing than ever before and Americans wondered, if they had been able to carry out those attacks, what would keep them from carrying out others in the near future.

To Get the Message Out

The hijackings on 9/11 were not only the perfect combination of symbolism and dramatic tactics, they also drew the media attention that is every terrorist's goal. The Council on Foreign Relations explains:

> Terrorists [tailor] their attacks to maximize publicity and get their messages out through all available channels. Experts say the attacks on the World Trade Center and the Pentagon, for example, were designed to provide billions of television viewers with pictures symbolizing U.S. vulnerability, and they prompted extensive reporting on al-Qaeda and its Islamist agenda.[25]

Terrorists want publicity for a number of reasons: first, so that the results of their actions will create panic, and second, so their organization can be recognized as a force that must be reckoned with. Publicity also helps the public better understand their cause, draws in sympathizers, and helps in fundraising. It can even give the terrorists themselves a chance to learn about countermeasures being taken against them.

Terrorists have known for decades that the media can be used to their advantage to get publicity. In the 1960s terrorists such as the Italian Red Brigades staged their attacks on Saturdays so they appeared in Sunday newspapers, which had higher circulation than other days of the week. The Palestinian group Black September took Israeli athletes hostage at the 1972 Olympics in part because millions of people were already watching the games on television. Timothy McVeigh stated that he chose the Murrah Federal Building in Oklahoma City because it had "plenty of open space around it, to allow for the best possible news photos and television footage."[26]

The World Trade Center in New York was destroyed by terrorist attacks on September 11, 2001.

News organizations always cover terrorist attacks. They are always looking for dramatic stories, and when a bombing or kidnapping occurs, hundreds of photographers and journalists are sent out to get the story, which becomes headline news.

Not surprisingly, the public is divided over whether the media ought to publicize the terrorists' activities. Those who believe they should not say that newspeople are simply being manipulated. They are giving terrorists attention they do not deserve. That attention could motivate them to prolong an event like a hostage situation in order to get more publicity. Or perhaps a newsperson's remarks could put pressure on law officials to respond to a situation prematurely, or could alert terrorists to rescue plans that are being formulated.

Those who believe that some good can come from the media publicizing terrorist activities emphasize that the public always has a right to know what is going on in the world. In addition, they point to a decision that several major American newspapers made (with the support of the U.S. Justice Department) in 1995. At that time the papers agreed to publish the manifesto of the Unabomber, Theodore Kaczynski, a lone terrorist who had eluded the FBI for seventeen years. In return, he promised to end his bombing campaign. After the manifesto was printed in the newspaper, Kaczynski's brother recognized elements of Theodore's writing style and contacted the authorities. The Unabomber was arrested in April 1996.

No matter whether publicity helps or hurts, the media has made terrorism more visible in many ways. The establishment of Arabic cable news television networks like Al-Jazeera and the development of video capabilities of the World Wide Web allow terrorists to film their messages

Solo terrorist Theodore Kaczynski, also known as the Unabomber, was arrested in April 1996 after a seventeen-year bombing spree.

and broadcast them to a variety of audiences. Journalist Rajat Madhok notes, "In order to attain maximum impact, terrorist groups have now become skilful at dealing with the media. They issue press releases, take part in news conferences and provide journalists with necessary background information."[27]

Not only has the media made terrorism more visible, it has allowed terrorists to reach out to the farthest parts of the world to recruit new members. One of the most popular methods of recruiting today is via the Internet, because almost everyone has access to this form of technology, and because it is virtually uncontrollable, allowing individuals to e-mail, enter chat rooms, or access Web sites freely and effortlessly. Technology expert Kevin LaGrandeur explains:

> Web sites set up to support terrorist and hate organizations are increasingly common. . . . These hate sites are essentially inexpensive billboards or, more accurately, propaganda machines planted where children and impressionable adults may find them. Their poisonous message is frightening because they are so cheap, easy to implement, immediate, and accessible.[28]

3

Terrorist Recruiting and Training

RECRUITING IS A vital part of terrorism that allows groups to grow, gain power, and accomplish their goals. A variety of techniques are used to attract and inform new members. Most groups target individuals in their early twenties, but for some, enlistment begins as early as the preschool years.

Once recruited, the newcomers must be trained and indoctrinated so they can function as effectively as possible. Often this merely involves playing up aspects of their personalities that are already prone to seeing terrorism as a valid way of approaching life's problems. In other cases, it involves a period of time in classes or a camp where participants learn everything from religious doctrine to weapons training.

Born into Terrorism

Some young people are virtually born into terrorism. In Palestinian refugee camps throughout the Middle East, for instance, schools ranging from kindergartens to high schools are run by Hamas, and students regularly see banners, recite slogans, and hear accounts of events that glorify violence against Israel and the West. Matthew A. Levitt writes of Hamas:

> The graduation ceremony at a kindergarten run by al-Jam'iya al-Islamiya, a Hamas charitable association, . . . featured 1,600 preschool age children wearing uniforms and carrying pretend rifles. A five-year-old girl reenacted attacks on Israelis by dipping her hands in red paint, mimicking the bloodied hands Palestinians proudly displayed after the lynching of two Israelis in [the Palestinian city of] Ramallah.[29]

The propaganda is backed by solid support. The humanitarian branch of Hamas provides food, clothing, and shelter to refugees. In contrast, Israeli Defense Forces (the Israeli military) seem evil as they demolish Palestinian homes and kill Palestinian men in revenge for previous terrorist strikes.

As a result, even young Palestinians like eleven-year-old Ahmed become angry, hate filled, and ready to carry out a terrorist attack without a second thought. Ahmed states: "I will make my body a bomb that will blast the flesh of Zionists [Israelis], the sons of pigs and monkeys. . . . I will tear their bodies into little pieces and cause them more pain than they will ever know."[30]

On-Campus Recruiting

While some like Ahmed are drawn into terrorism as children, most are not recruited until they are young adults. If they are Muslim, this could take place at a mosque or other Muslim meeting place. There they may turn to terrorism after hearing a radical speaker who persuades them to embrace fundamentalism and jihad.

Terrorist groups try to indoctrinate their followers at an early age. These Palestinian children hold toy guns and chant in support of the terrorist group Hamas.

Islamic schools known as madrassas are good recruiting centers as well, because these schools teach Islam from a fundamentalist point of point of view. This usually portrays the West as the enemy of Muslims and a force of evil to be hated and defeated. Students are exposed to the teachings and writings of Islamic radicals such as Abdallah Azzam, who influenced Osama bin Laden and many others to take part in terrorism. Abu Bakar University in Karachi, Pakistan, is an example of such a fundamentalist madrassa. In addition to teaching the Koran, Islamic literature, and Arabic, it is closely affiliated with the fundamentalist Ahle-Hadith movement and the Islamic terrorist group Lashkar-e-Taiba, thus providing students with connections to these organizations.

Terrorist recruiters can be found even at traditional universities. This is because campuses are centers where people from all over the world gather and all kinds of ideas are exchanged. Young people who take part in these exchanges are often idealistic, impatient with government shortcomings, eager to embrace new ideas, and ready for action. Many of them are likely to be open to recruiters' persuasiveness.

Terrorists are quick to realize this and take advantage of invitations to visit universities. In 2003, for instance, members of ecoterrorist groups such as the Earth Liberation Front (ELF) and the Animal Liberation Front (ALF) were among speakers at a two-day conference hosted by the Political Science Department at California State University, Fresno. Attendees heard about the abuse animals and the environment face at the hands of biomedical researchers, fur farmers, land developers, and others. They also learned about "direct action" techniques—arson, vandalism of new construction, and so on— that they could take to counter such abuse. No numbers were available regarding new recruits at the end of the seminar.

Other Recruiting Sites

Like universities, prisons are sites where young men are recruited into terrorism. Many prisoners are already angry, frustrated, and ready to do violence. Some are bored and willing to listen to fellow inmates who have become Muslims, and who preach the notion of overcoming oppression through jihad. After becoming militants in prison, they are ready to join a terrorist organization when they are released.

One well-known terrorist who was converted to Islam while in prison was Richard Reid, the so-called shoe bomber. Reid became a follower of the Muslim faith while in Feltham Young Offenders' Institution in West London. Intending to blow up an airliner, he was caught with explosives in his sneakers while en route to the United States in December 2001.

Although prisons and schools are viable recruiting grounds, terrorist-sponsored media reaches a wider audience and is often the first place that recruits hear about a terrorist organization. Hizballah, for instance, has its own television and radio stations and a variety of Web sites, which provide the latest information on activities the organization offers, inspirational messages from its leaders, and accounts of its achievements. It also publishes two magazines, *al-Intiqad* and *Baqiatollah*, which give a proterrorist slant to the political and religious matters they discuss. All of this draws in the curious, then directs those who show interest to other people who can tell them more.

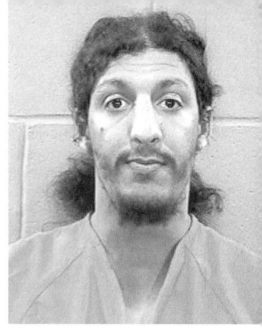

British passenger Richard Reid hid explosives in his sneakers in a thwarted attempt to blow up an American Airlines Boeing 767 in midair in December 2001.

"Professional" Terrorists

Recruiting efforts draw in all kinds of people who are willing to support terrorism. Some do not want to carry out violent acts, but will give money to an organization. Some are willing to provide safe houses in which agents can stay while they carry out an attack. Some will work at legitimate businesses that act as fronts for terrorism; that is, the money brought in is used for terrorism.

Some recruits, however, go on to become full-time "professional" terrorists. These are men and women who dedicate their lives to terrorist causes, have positions of leadership in terrorist organizations, and help plan attacks, recruit, raise funds, or fill other positions of importance. They are usually highly intelligent individuals who have above-average reasoning skills. Osama bin Laden is the epitome of such a terrorist.

Journalist Rohan Gunaratna describes him: "He is patient, cunning and deceptive. The planning and preparations to attack the U.S. embassies in East Africa lasted five years. . . . Additionally, he has the capacity to plan several operations simultaneously."[31]

The Terrorist Personality

Most professional terrorists have certain personality traits in common, traits that experts have determined to be atypical and antisocial. The first trait is a fanatic loyalty to a cause, often a religious one. Such people are not attracted to moderate viewpoints, and when they have adopted their extremist views, they become intent on carrying them to their logical conclusions. Christian fundamentalist terrorist Shelley Shannon of Oregon is an example. Shannon became involved in Operation Rescue and the Army of God, antiabortion groups who believe that abortion is murder. She began corresponding with other right-wing radicals, who encouraged her conviction that allowing abortion doctors to live was, in essence, condoning murder. She went on to bomb six abortion clinics in 1992 and attempted to kill physician George Tiller in 1993, knowing there was a good chance she would be apprehended for the crimes. Unwilling to abandon her cause, however, she did what she believed was the will of God and is currently serving a thirty-one-year term in prison.

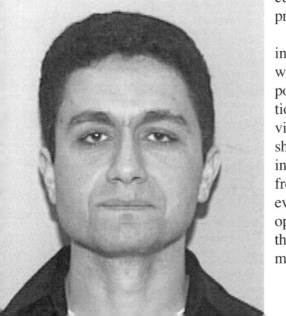

Mohammed Atta was one of the ringleaders of the September 11, 2001, terrorist attacks on New York and Washington, D.C.

Another trait that terrorists exhibit is thinking in terms of absolutes. They believe that what they think is right and any differing viewpoint is wrong. This logically leads to the notion that the person with the "wrong" viewpoint is bad. For terrorists, there are no shades of gray in a situation. They cannot step into the other person's shoes or see the world from another person's point of view. Thus, everyone who differs from them becomes their opponent, and, rather than trying to convert that opponent to a different way of thinking, many terrorists prefer to eliminate him or her entirely. Once such people are eliminated, the terrorist feels no guilt or remorse for their deaths because he or she has not understood or identified with them in any way. The terrorist has only seen them as enemies.

Another trait terrorists exhibit is close-minded certainty. They believe that what they are doing is right and they have no doubts or second thoughts. Once they have made up their minds, they also cannot be persuaded that they are wrong, and no amount of fear will make them stop what they are going to do. Thus they are good candidates for carrying out a terrorist attack, even if it is very dangerous. Two notes left behind by Mohammed Atta, one of the September 11 attackers, illustrate this. The first states: "Everybody hates death, fears death, but only those, the believers who know the life after death and the reward after death, would be the ones who will be seeking death." The second, a short memo, says: "Check your weapon, say morning prayer together, and, if you take a taxi to the airport, when you arrive, smile and rest assured, for Allah is with the believers and the angels are protecting you."[32]

Those who knew Atta testify that he exhibited yet another trait that many terrorists possess—he had difficulty fitting into normal society. Because they are intense, extremely serious, and aloof, such people find it difficult to make friends. In a terrorist organization, however, they find others who are like them. Everyone has a shared sense of identity and a purpose in life. Everyone thinks the same. Thus the organization is very attractive, especially to those who felt lonely and purposeless before joining. Psychologist Peter M. Forster notes that "social networks are important in the recruitment of new members into violent Islamic fundamentalist groups, including al Qaeda. . . . Biographical data for over 400 members of such groups . . . [showed] that about 70% of terrorists had joined while they were living as expatriates [emigrants] in other countries, looking for jobs and education."[33]

Fatal Choices

Suicide bombers are like other terrorists in that they are intense, serious individuals who are fanatically loyal to a cause, think in terms of absolutes, and exhibit close-minded certainty. A vast majority are young. All are angry and believe that the group they represent is being repressed or ignored by governments in power. Unlike individuals who commit suicide because of depression or other mental problems, however, most suicide bombers view their act as an exciting strike against the enemy, and they take great pride in being strong, focused, and determined when they perform their deadly activities.

Once a suicide bomber has made the decision to give his or her life for a terrorist cause, others in the group rally around to support the decision—and to ensure he or she does not have a change of heart. First, all ties to the outside world are severed. Only on the eve of the event can the bombers see their families for a short time. Then, they are surrounded by advisers who bolster their courage and mentally prepare them for the attack. They are given countless hours of intense spiritual training, instructed in the details of jihad, and reminded how sweet revenge on the enemy will be. At no time are they allowed an opportunity for second thoughts. Jerold Post of George Washington University observes, "From the time they were recruited, the group never left their sides, leaving them no opportunity of backing down from their fatal choice."[34]

Rich Rewards

During the preparation process, the bombers are also treated with great honor and respect. They are praised repeatedly for the rich rewards they will bring to their families because of their sacrifice. Immediately after the bombing, for instance, parents become the guests of honor at celebrations that are much like wedding receptions. Many have their debts paid off or receive generous pensions for life. Some are given new homes, new cars, or cash.

Bombers are also reminded of the rewards they can look forward to in heaven after death. "A river of honey, a river of wine and 72 virgins. Since I have been studying Koran I know about the sweet life that waits there (in Paradise),"[35] one aspiring suicide bomber said.

"More Advanced than Training"

Many details are known about al Qaeda training camps in Afghanistan, where at least five thousand recruits, including at least four of the nineteen 9/11 hijackers, received training in the 1990s. Of the dozens of facilities that Osama bin Laden established there, Zhawar Khili, Khalden, and Darunta were three of the best known. In Khalden, one hundred men could train in everything from hand-to-hand combat to bomb construction. At Darunta, chemical weapons research was carried out on dogs, rabbits, and other animals.

During their 2002 invasion of Afghanistan, U.S. troops found Taliban and al Qaeda weapons hidden in caves along with pro–bin Laden posters in al Qaeda classrooms.

Most of the camps also had weight-training facilities, obstacle courses, and shooting ranges where targets were cutouts of Americans. In one camp trainers replicated a small Western-style city on a hillside so trainees could

practice destroying houses, office buildings, and bridges. "It is more advanced than training," says Gunaratna. "It is almost like doing the operation so that when they go to the real operational theater, they will be a hundred percent confident."[36]

At the al Qaeda camps, students spent a great deal of time on religious study, but they also took classes on the best places to hide bombs on airplanes, were given step-by-step instructions on how to use surface-to-air missiles, and practiced hostage taking and assassination techniques. The most promising recruits were also provided with a special manual entitled *Declaration of Jihad: The Military Series*, which provided in-depth training on special missions they might undertake. The book covered in great detail everything from renting safe apartments to wearing the right clothes while spying on the enemy. "They are really training for specific missions," terrorist expert Magnus Ranstorp emphasizes. "And it's weeding out the elite of the elite, the crème de la crème, who may be deployed for even more specialized training, to even maybe be deployed [to] the West for terrorist purposes."[37]

Although bombing campaigns during the war in Afghanistan effectively destroyed these camps, new ones were soon reestablished deep in the mountains of Pakistan and Afghanistan beyond the reach of American, Afghan, and Pakistani troops. At least one camp was reportedly established in Bosnia as well.

Centers of Terrorist Activities

Unlike the remote training camps set up by al Qaeda, training carried out by Hamas and Hizballah often takes place within the confines of the large Palestinian refugee camps that have existed for decades in southern Lebanon, on the West Bank, and in Gaza. Here, trainers and trainees meet, plan, and teach new recruits to use various weapons, assemble explosive devices, and devise suicide bombing attacks. Their activities are masked by the everyday activities of the community. They are thus undetected by authorities such as United Nations Relief and Works Agency, which administers the camps but does not take responsibility for security. Middle East expert Arlene Kushner states,

As a consequence of this situation, the . . . refugee camps have become centers of terrorist activities. It is often in the camps that terrorists are recruited, trained, and dispatched, and weapons manufactured; camps . . . are utilized for hiding terrorists and weapons. Camps provide a safe haven for terrorists from outside, while residents of the camps themselves are involved in terrorist activities.[38]

New recruits learn paramilitary skills at terrorist training camps like this one run by the Fatah Revolutionary Council, a militant Palestinian group.

Most of those who train in the refugee camps are usually sent into Israel, where some of them become suicide bombers. Others are trained to use mortars and short-range rockets against hard targets. Former Hamas leader Salah Shehada explained in 2002, "We define the target and the nature of the assault on it, whether it is a settlement, a military post, a military vehicle, or anything else. . . . After the target is approved, the martyrdom operation's perpetrator is trained. . . . Then the operation is ready to go."[39]

Planning and training are essential to any terrorist organization. Part of that planning involves budgeting for the many expenses the group has to deal with. Before 2001, terrorists had no problem in that respect because donors were abundant and generous. Due to the war on terror, however, terrorists have had to become more creative in order to hide their financial activities from authorities who are determined to stop the flow of money no matter where it originates and where it ends.

4

Financing Terrorism

ALTHOUGH A SINGLE terrorist attack requires only a few thousand dollars to carry out, the costs of running a terrorist organization over time are significant. There are endless expenses, including the cost of feeding a large group of recruits, purchasing weapons and ammunition, providing transportation such as cars or airline tickets, renting safe houses for operatives going on a mission, and a host of other items that quickly add up to a significant total. "Maintaining a terrorist cell can be very expensive,"[40] notes Jeff Breinholt, deputy chief of the Department of Justice counterterrorism section.

Terrorist organizations as a whole raise about $1.2 trillion a year from a variety of sources—usually donations from individuals and groups, from governments that sponsor terror, or from crime. Hizballah draws its support from all of these sources. The organization reportedly has an annual budget of somewhere between $220 and $500 million. About $120 million comes from the Iranian government. Substantial amounts come from Muslim communities, businesses, independent charities, and other organizations. Money from drug trafficking, counterfeiting, credit card forgery, and car theft makes up another noteworthy amount.

The sources of funding for any terrorist group are often so well disguised that it is impossible to trace exactly where the money comes from, how much comes in, and how it is spent. This has always been the case with al Qaeda. Although the organization has been the focus of counterterrorism since 2001 and can no longer amass the $30 million it once raised annually, it still manages to find secret sources of money that baffle the scrutiny of the most vigilant regulators. Lee Hamilton, vice chairman of the National Commission on Terrorist Attacks upon the United States, notes, "Despite our efforts, it appears that al-Qaeda can still find money to fund terrorist operations."[41]

Individuals and Organizations

Of the three categories of terrorist financing, money from individuals, organizations, and businesses has been a solid source of support for most groups in the past. One individual who has allegedly given millions of his own fortune is Saudi businessman Yassin A. Kadi, described by U.S. Treasury general counsel David Aufhauser as having "a long history of financing and facilitating the activities of terrorists and terrorist-related organizations, often acting through seemingly legitimate charitable enterprises and businesses."[42] Kadi is

Terrorist organizations have global connections. Twenty-two apartment units in these twin towers in Albania were used to support the activities of al Qaeda.

also the founder of the Muwafaq ("Blessed Relief") Foundation, an Islamic charity that employed or served as cover for a number of Islamic extremists connected with Bin Laden and other terror groups.

Terrorists appreciate wealthy individuals like Kadi, but organizations offer a greater amount of support because they are composed of large numbers of people who may give less individually but more in total. Charities and humanitarian groups range from American associations such as the Irish Northern Aid Committee (NORAID), which has links to the IRA and its offshoots, to the LTTE-affiliated Tamil Rehabilitation Organization, and the World Assembly of Muslim Youth, a Saudi-sponsored charity. Due to carelessness or ignorance, some contributors never check to see if these organizations and others like them are reputable and legitimate, and thus have no idea that their money is being spent on terrorist activities. They donate, expecting that their money will be used to help those in need. Instead of food or clothing, however, it is used to buy guns and bombs. As Treasury Department spokeswoman Molly Millerwise notes, "In many cases donors are being unwittingly misled."[43] Other donors, however, understand how their money is being used and are comfortable being passive supporters of terrorism because they agree with the philosophy of the organization if not its outright use of violence.

Businesses

Most businesses that support terrorism are well aware that they are fronting terrorism. Usually, the business is legal and merely diverts some of its profits to a terrorist organization. An example of this was the Beit al-Mal Holding Company, a public investment company with offices in East Jerusalem, the West Bank, and the Gaza Strip. Its stated business was making loans and investing in economic and social development projects, but the majority of its shareholders, founders, and employees were associated with Hamas, and it supported many Hamas activities. On December 4, 2001, acting under the authority of Executive Order 13224, Blocking Terrorist Property, the Bush administration froze its assets—stopped it from carrying out financial transactions—stating that it was responsible for financing terror.

Sometimes a business is set up specifically to be an arm of a terrorist organization. Such was the case with the Al-Taqwa Management Group, created in 1988 by the Muslim Brotherhood (a predecessor of militant groups such as Hamas and Islamic Jihad) to move and safeguard large quantities of cash for terrorist causes. Bush explained in 2001, "Al-Taqwa is an association of offshore banks and financial management firms that have helped al-Qaeda shift money around the world."[44] The group, which changed its name to Nada Management Organization in the spring of 2000 after authorities began an investigation into its dealings, is headquartered in Lugano, Switzerland. Representatives deny any involvement in terrorist activities, but the U.S. government froze its assets in November 2001.

State Sponsors

Al Qaeda and other terrorists often carry out business transactions in countries such as Switzerland, Saudi Arabia, Norway, and others whose laws are relaxed when it comes to registering charities, providing identification when opening bank accounts, and so forth. They have closer ties however, with governments that actually sponsor terrorism—that is, those that support terrorists financially and use them as a way of waging secret war against their enemies. Such governments include those of Cuba, Libya, North Korea, Syria, Sudan, and Iran.

Iran has been considered the most active state sponsor of terrorism for many years. Its government, which became a fundamentalist Islamic theocracy led by conservative ayatollahs in 1979, not only makes funding and weapons available to a variety of Islamic groups, it provides training and offers sanctuary to terrorist groups as well. Some of them include Hizballah (which it helped found in the 1980s), Hamas, and Palestinian Islamic Jihad (a branch of Egyptian Islamic Jihad). It also provides safe haven for members of Ansar al Islam (a Kurdish terrorist group in northern Iraq) and to other militant groups in the Persian Gulf region, Africa, and Central Asia.

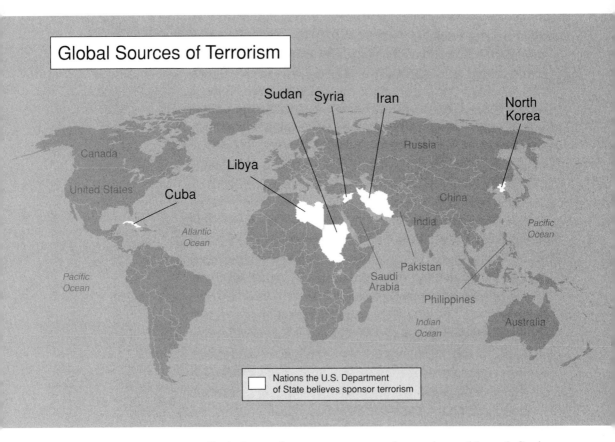

Global Sources of Terrorism

Sudan   Syria   Iran

North Korea

Libya

Canada

Russia

United States

Cuba

China

Atlantic Ocean

India

Pacific Ocean

Pacific Ocean

Pakistan

Saudi Arabia

Philippines

Indian Ocean

Australia

Nations the U.S. Department of State believes sponsor terrorism

Syria is another state sponsor of terrorism, although Syrian officials are careful to distinguish between terrorism and what they view as legitimate resistance against Israel. Government leaders have cooperated with the United States against al Qaeda and other extremist Islamic terrorist groups, and have made efforts to limit the movement of anticoalition fighters into Iraq during the war that began in 2003. They provide support for Palestinian terrorists such as Hizballah, however, allow it to operate out of their country, and according to the U.S. Department of State, provide it with "substantial amounts of financial, training, weapons, explosives, political, diplomatic, and organizational aid."[45] They also allow Iranian weapons bound for Hizballah to regularly pass through their country, and, when they occupied and controlled Lebanon between 1990 and 2005, they let Hizballah operate in Lebanon and attack Israel.

Syria has also provided training, weapons, safe haven, and logistical support to other groups that fight against Israel. The Popular Front for the Liberation of Palestine–General Command (a splinter group of the Popular Front for the Liberation of Palestine) and the Palestinian Islamic Jihad have their headquarters in Damascus. Other terrorist groups, including Hamas, have offices there as well.

In the latter part of the twentieth century, Libya was also one of the world's most dangerous sponsors of terrorism. In 2003, however, Libyan president Muammar Qaddafi announced that he was willing to allow international inspectors into the country to dismantle his arsenal of weaponry. It is believed that, after Saddam Hussein's regime was overthrown, Qaddafi feared for his own future. Inspectors found several thousand tons of chemical weapons, as well as an active nuclear weapons program. The process of destroying the weapons is ongoing, and Libya has improved its cooperation with international monitoring agencies. The country will officially remain a state sponsor of terrorism, however, until it has fully broken all ties with terrorist groups and has proven that it has permanently halted the use of violence for political purposes.

Criminal Activities

With their funding cut due to war and Western intervention, terrorist groups need the ability to stock their treasuries from other sources. Thus, most also rely on criminal activities that can range from illicit trade in diamonds and precious metals to human trafficking that includes prostitution and/or slavery.

For FARC, drug trafficking is a significant source of income. About 330 tons (300 metric tons) of cocaine are smuggled into the United States each year, and approximately 80 to 90 percent of that is shipped from Colombia. The U.S. Drug Enforcement Administration estimates that FARC controls approximately 70 percent of the Colombian cocaine trade. It is involved in all aspects of the trade and also extorts protection money from coca plantation owners and processors (who grow and produce cocaine) and from other drug traffickers to allow them to use secret airstrips, aircraft, and so on. These

The guerrilla fighters of the Revolutionary Armed Forces of Colombia (FARC) are considered terrorists by the Colombian government.

activities help the organization buy weapons, ammunition, and equipment necessary to carry out violent attacks against Colombian political, military, and economic targets.

While FARC relies on drug trafficking, the LTTE operates a huge network of criminal fund-raising that stretches from Canada to Australia. Its activities range from arms smuggling to prostitution, extortion, and fraud. In 2000, for instance, the organization attempted to push through a scheme in which Canada Post would print a stamp in remembrance of Kumar Ponnambalam, a Tamil boy who died in a shoot-out in Toronto in 1999. A portion of the revenue collected from the sale of the stamp would go to the Toronto police. The rest would go to a group called the United Tamils. Investigation revealed, however, that Ponnambalam was in reality a LTTE attorney, and the United Tamils was a LTTE organization.

The Sri Lankan government reports: "The attempt to get the Police involved under the guise of community work seems to have been an attempt by the LTTE to use the Canadian Police as a cover for their racket."[46]

Hamas raises money from a variety of criminal activities that include counterfeiting and credit card theft. One is that of cigarette smuggling, also known as cigarette diversion. This illegal venture, which has its basis in tax evasion, is easy and lucrative, and takes place even in the United States. The smugglers buy a large volume of cigarettes in a state where the tax is low—Virginia or North Carolina, for instance—then transport them to a state with higher taxes, such as New York. There they sell them to small mom-and-pop businesses or out of the back of a car at a discount rate that still nets them a good profit because the smugglers never pay the higher taxes in that state. The profit on a carton can be about $40, and smugglers can make about $2 million on a single truckload of cigarettes. "The schemes provide terrorists millions of dollars which can be used to purchase firearms and explosives to use against the United States and others,"[47] said Carl J. Truscott, director of the Bureau of Alcohol, Tobacco, Firearms, and Explosives, in 2004.

Shell Companies and Money Laundering

Because authorities worldwide are on the lookout for funds being raised, spent, or transferred illegally or for terrorist purposes, terrorists take pains to hide their financial transactions so that even the smartest authorities have trouble finding them. Institute for Counter-Terrorism researcher Yael Shahar wrote in 2001,

> In an attempt to find out who bankrolled the attacks on New York and Washington, U.S. investigators [had] to examine electronic banking systems and known offshore banking havens. They [also sought] the cooperation of authorities in Malaysia, Singapore and other Asian countries where bin Laden is believed to have established bank accounts and "shell companies."[48]

Shell companies are companies that have no assets or operations. Because they can be totally inactive or used as fronts for other organizations, terrorists can hold, hide, or channel money through them under the guise of salaries, expenses, and income.

Shell companies are only one way that terrorists try to throw authorities off their trail as they use money for their violent purposes. Another method they use to disguise the origins of the money they raise is called "laundering"—so called because it cleans up the money's "dirty" origins and gets it into the legitimate financial system.

A criminal's need to launder money is based on the fact that, in the United States at least, cash transactions and deposits of more than $10,000 have to be reported to the Financial Crimes Enforcement Network, along with any other suspicious financial activity. Criminal transactions are often carried out in cash, which is harder to trace than checks or credit cards. Thus, if a criminal takes in large amounts of cash from the sale of drugs, the smuggling of cigarettes, or the like he or she has to launder it. One way to do this is to give it to an associate who is already taking in large amounts of cash, usually as part of a legally declared business. The associate deposits the money into his or her own account and writes a check for that amount back to the criminal. As a result, the criminal can deposit the check into his or her bank account without drawing attention to him- or herself.

Another method of laundering money involves giving small amounts of cash to several confederates who then use that money to purchase goods for the criminal—anything from diamonds to tourist items. Those goods can then be sold again or shipped out of the country. The origin of the goods becomes clouded, and the fact that goods have been purchased with "dirty" money becomes hard to prove.

Alternative Financial Systems

In many cases, terrorists do not have to launder money, they simply have to secretly transfer and distribute clean money or valuables that have been contributed to their illegal cause. One way they transfer valuables is by smuggling things in ingenious places such as frozen fish or bulk shipments of vegetables. These are then shipped out of the country and picked up in another country by the terrorists' associates.

HOLY LAND FOUNDATION

The most popular way of transferring money is by using "alternative financial systems" also known as "parallel" or "underground" financial systems, which make anonymous transfers of funds relatively easy. Although such systems can be used for legitimate purposes, they are also used to funnel money to and from terrorist groups all over the world. Alvin James, a specialist in money laundering investigation, states,

> There are major similarities among all underground financial systems. . . . The most significant of these similarities is their ability to facilitate anonymous international transfers of money. This feature makes these systems attractive to terrorist groups. We know that they use these systems to covertly move the money they need to support their activities.[49]

One alternative financial system is the Colombia Black Market Peso Exchange, the largest system in the Western Hemisphere. It is used by Colombian drug lords and terrorists who need to be able to securely change U.S. currency to pesos and get it out of the United States without going through legally regulated financial systems. Other alternative

The U.S. government shut down the Holy Land Foundation (HLF) because of its ties to terrorist groups. HLF CEO Ghassen Elashi (speaking) was arrested on December 18, 2002.

systems are the *hawala* or "chit" systems, which are widely used in the Middle East and Asia. These systems are virtually paperless schemes. Instead of signing contracts and keeping written records, participants use verbal agreements, handshakes, code words, or digitally encrypted messages to keep track of and seal their deals.

For instance, an individual in the United States wanting to transfer several thousand dollars to a terrorist in Pakistan contacts a *hawaladar* (agent) in the United States who takes the money and, for a small fee, calls or e-mails a *hawaladar* in Pakistan, usually a relative or someone who owes money to the U.S. *hawaladar*. This Pakistani arranges delivery of the money to the terrorist in a timely fashion, with the amount deducted from the Pakistani's debt. No records other than a phone bill or e-mail are kept of the transaction; the entire proceeding is informal and is based on trust that all the parties involved will do what they say. The fact that everyone has confidence in each other's reliability is what makes the system work so well. Financial crimes experts Harjit Singh Sandhu and Patrick M. Jost note, "The components of hawala that distinguish it from other remittance systems are trust and the extensive use of connections such as family relationships or regional affiliations."[50]

Putting together all the pieces of the complex financial puzzle that terrorists have set up to guard their funding has proven one of the most challenging aspects of the war on terror. The difficulties are never ending, because just as one financier is arrested, one law is rewritten, or one source is shut down, the terrorists find a new ally, a new loophole, or a new hiding place that allows them to continue their efforts. Nevertheless, the counterterrorism quest continues. Officials realize that only by cutting off terrorism at

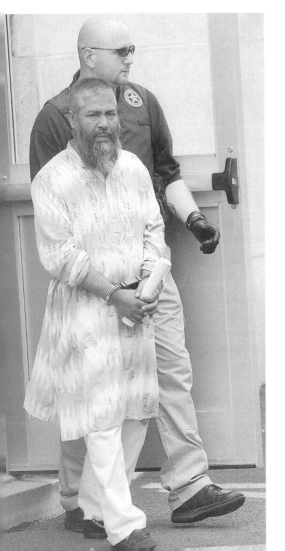

In August 2004 the FBI raided a mosque in Albany, New York, suspected of connections to terrorist organizations. A founder of the mosque, Mohammed Hossain, was arrested.

its roots will the world ever be free of men like Osama bin Laden, Hizballah head Hassan Nasrallah, and others. "In the game of prevention," says Jeff Breinholt of the U.S. Department of Justice, "it is not enough to expect law enforcement will uncover the bomber before he detonates the bomb. The goal of pursuing terrorism financing . . . is to widen the universe of possible criminal defendants so that we can prosecute before the terrorist act occurs."[51]

5

Counterterrorism

WHEN BUSH DECLARED war on terrorism in 2001, he knew that the world would be fighting terrorists on a long-term basis. Thus, he and his allies worked to develop a wide range of counterterrorism strategies that could be effective for years to come. These included building strong, modern armies; having tight homeland security; cutting off terrorist financing; and promoting freedom and democracy around the world. "The more frequently and relentlessly we strike the terrorists across all fronts, using all the tools of statecraft, the more effective we will be,"[52] Bush stated in his National Strategy for Combating Terrorism, published in 2003.

Using the Military

Modernizing the military was the first counterterrorism strategy adopted by Western nations after 9/11. Shortly after the attacks, the Bush administration significantly increased military spending, helped push to make the military a more flexible and lethal force, and instituted changes so that it could more easily interact with U.S. intelligence agencies as well as other nations' military and intelligence systems.

The United States and its allies also helped transform other agencies such as the North Atlantic Treaty Organization (NATO) to make them more effective at fighting terrorism in the twenty-first century. (NATO is an international organization created in 1949 for purposes of collective security. Its members include the United States, Canada, and most European countries.) Today, for instance, NATO has established Operation Active Endeavour, a terrorism-monitoring and identification presence in the Mediterranean Sea. It also has an early warning and control aircraft that can detect terrorists that may attack from the skies, as well as a chemical-radiological-nuclear defense battalion that offers assessment, advice, and leadership for other units who are dealing with the potential presence of weapons of mass destruction. "This new unit is a superb symbol of the transformed NATO," says NATO secretary general Lord George Islay MacNeill Robertson. "We will see 15 NATO countries . . . working together to provide a high-tech multinational solution to today's threats."[53]

U.S. forces have detained many people in Afghanistan suspected of being members of the Taliban or al Qaeda. Here, an unidentified Afghani man is being taken into custody.

In the months after the attacks on the World Trade Center and the Pentagon, a coalition of military forces from nations including the United States, Britain, and France joined to help topple the fundamentalist Taliban regime that protected Osama bin Laden in Afghanistan. By 2003 Bin Laden was in hiding, the Taliban was out of power, and progress was made in breaking up terrorist rings around the world. Saudi Arabian legal and military officials thwarted attacks, arrested hundreds of suspects, and captured large amounts of explosives and weapons. The Israeli Defense Forces increased their retaliatory attacks against suicide bombers by bombing homes of suspected terrorists and killing militant leaders like Salah Shehada, head of Palestinian Hamas, and Mekled Hameid, a top Palestinian Islamic Jihad commander. These two terrorists were responsible for hundreds of attacks and bombings against Israeli civilians in recent years.

In other instances, government and military officials in Pakistan and Yemen cooperated with the United States to track down and capture terrorists such as Ramzi Binalshibh, an alleged coordinator of the September 11 attacks and attacks on the USS *Cole*, and Khalid Sheikh Mohammed, the alleged mastermind of the 9/11 attacks who had also conspired in the kidnapping of reporter Daniel Pearl. As a result of such instances of cooperation, more than two-thirds of the senior al Qaeda leaders, operational managers, and key facilitators sought by the United States had been captured or killed by October 2004.

In 2003 a different coalition of armies led by the U.S. military also helped topple Saddam Hussein's Baathist regime in Iraq. Hussein, who was known to provide support to terrorists and was believed to have been hiding weapons of mass destruction, was captured by U.S. forces in December 2003.

After the September 11, 2001, terrorist attacks, U.S. airport security was tightened and baggage and passenger searches increased.

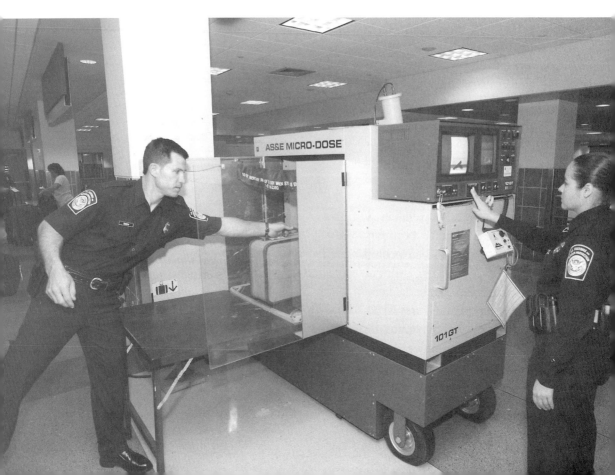

During the course of the war, hundreds of terrorists, including senior operatives who were part of Jordanian terrorist Abu Musab al Zarqawi's insurgency movement, were captured as well. Al Zarqawi was a supporter of Osama bin Laden and was responsible for much of the violence that took place in Iraq after Hussein's regime fell.

Homeland Security

While the military fought terrorism abroad, the Bush administration worked to strengthen America's defenses at home. The Office of Homeland Security was created in 2001 and the Department of Homeland Security in 2003, both specifically designed to prevent another terrorist strike on American soil.

Airport security was the first to be addressed. Federal agents were hired to screen passengers and luggage for weapons and explosives. Bulletproof, attack-proof cockpit doors were installed to keep pilots safe. Air marshals, alert for trouble, rode on many commercial flights. To address the concern that terrorists might shoot airliners out of the sky, the Department of Homeland Security planned to begin installing and testing a high-tech missile defense system on a few commercial planes in the United States at the end of 2005. The system was designed to find and disable missiles before they could strike planes.

Border security was a second focal point. Inspection hours were lengthened at checkpoints, more guards were hired, and inspection procedures became more intense. Agreements such as a Border Partnership Action Plan that focused on protecting the U.S. infrastructure and securing the flow of people and goods into the country were formed with neighboring countries. In 2002 Congress passed the Enhanced Border Security and Visa Entry Reform Act (also known as the Border Security Act). By the end of 2005, citizens of countries that were part of a visa waiver program were required to have new tamper-resistant, machine-readable passports that would help deter fraud and confirm the passport holder's identity quickly.

Port security was also addressed. The Container Security Initiative focused on prescreening cargo in twenty foreign countries before it reached American shores. The Coast

Guard's Underwater Port Security System (UPSS) was unveiled in March 2005. It was designed to detect, track, and stop underwater intruders, as well as inspect ships and piers. Petty Officer First Class Amy Thomas explains, "[The UPSS] adds an additional layer of protection to our ports, and is available in the US anywhere and anytime."[54] In April 2005 the Port of Oakland, California, became the first deepwater port in the United States to be able to automatically scan all inbound cargo ships for radioactive material that might indicate the presence of a nuclear device. Other ports planned to follow in its footsteps in the near future.

Law Enforcement Aids

To aid law enforcement in their pursuit of terrorists, Congress passed the Patriot Act on October 25, 2001. This act allowed FBI agents to access private information such as medical records, library records, student records, and such in their efforts to identify and catch terrorists. In the new age of cellphones, it also granted them the use of special "roving" wiretaps that would follow an individual rather than a phone number, and allowed terrorist suspects to be held in jail for longer periods of time without being brought to trial if an investigation proved complex or slow moving.

Law enforcement and intelligence agencies also began cooperating more extensively to identify domestic terror suspects and prevent them from striking. In 2002, for instance, white supremacist William Krar of Texas was arrested after a package containing fake Department of Defense ID badges was delivered to the wrong address and police were notified. Dozens of law enforcement agencies became involved in tracking the perpetrator, among them the FBI, who traced the package to Krar and discovered a sodium cyanide bomb large enough to kill everyone inside a 30,000-square-foot (2,787 sq m) building. Krar had also accumulated an arsenal of machine guns, explosives and ammunition. "This case was very high priority [for all of us],"[55] said Brit Featherson, assistant U.S. attorney in charge of the case.

Catching those involved in international terrorism in the United States continued to be top priority for authorities, too.

In 2002 Texan white supremacist William Krar was arrested for the illegal possession of machine guns and explosives.

Based on information gleaned from captured al Qaeda leader Khalid Sheikh Mohammad, federal agents took into custody Ali al-Marri, an alleged al Qaeda operative who had lived in Illinois for many years. Al-Marri had planned to blow up bridges, dams, and railroads in the United States. In June 2002, on the basis of information they gained from another senior al Qaeda commander who was in American custody, the FBI arrested Jose Padilla, a former gang member from Brooklyn, on charges of plotting a dirty-bomb strike in the United States on behalf of al Qaeda.

After FBI agents caught national guardsman Ryan Anderson attempting to provide intelligence to al Qaeda on an undercover video, he was found guilty of attempting to aid and provide intelligence to the enemy in September 2004. In May 2005 Pennsylvania resident Ronald Grecula was also arrested by the FBI and charged with offering to build and sell a bomb to an affiliate of al Qaeda. FBI agents recorded telephone conversations he had with a confidential source, and then took him into custody after he agreed to sell undercover officers a bomb. "He was acting to get some type of revenge against the United States or at least enable other people to get revenge against the U.S. . . . If it looks like he's taking action . . . we're not going to wait for him to prove he can do it successfully,"[56] said U.S. attorney Michael Shelby.

Cutting Off the Money

Identifying, tracking, and interfering with the flow of money to al Qaeda and other terrorist groups was as vital a part of the war on terrorism as was catching terrorists. The United States

At the urging of the U.S. government, Saudi Arabia shut down the Al Haramain Islamic Foundation in 2004 because of its connections to terrorist organizations.

and its allies believed that those who supported terror with their money were just as guilty of terrorism as those who detonated bombs or crashed airplanes. In addition, the faster financial networks were shut down, the less money there would be to buy bombs and train operatives to detonate them.

To that end, in 2001 the Financial Action Task Force, an intergovernmental body that develops national and international policies to combat money laundering and terrorist financing, issued recommendations to help countries put an end to the financing of terrorism. Some of those recommendations included criminalizing the financing of terrorism; freezing and confiscating terrorist assets; imposing anti-money-laundering requirements on alternative financing systems; and ensuring that businesses and organizations, in particular nonprofit organizations, could not be misused to finance terrorism.

Most countries were willing to cooperate. At least 173 issued orders to freeze terrorist assets, to prevent them from making financial transactions such as transferring money from one bank account to another. More than 100 introduced new legislation to fight terrorist financing in various ways. More than 80 established financial intelligence units to share information. The United States blocked some $36 million in assets of terrorist entities and supporters; other nations blocked more than $100 million in terrorists' assets.

Some countries, however, needed to be pressured to take necessary steps. Such was the case with the Saudi Arabian government and a charity known as the Al Haramain Islamic Foundation. While Al Haramain was committed to providing educational, financial, and material support to poor Muslims, it had been infiltrated by terrorist supporters who were siphoning money and materials to al Qaeda. For four years the Saudi government resisted shutting it down. Finally, in 2004, after lengthy discussions with U.S. officials, the Saudi government announced it would dissolve the charity's operations. "I think the action . . . was an important one. It was far-reaching. It indicates [Saudi] seriousness-[in]-dealing with the issue of terrorism finance,"[57] says U.S. treasury secretary John Snow.

Offshore Banks

Another way that authorities cut off money to terrorists was through regulation of offshore financial centers (OFCs), more commonly known as offshore banks. OFCs are located throughout the world, often on islands like the Bahamas or the Caymans, or in countries like Monaco or Liechtenstein.

Before 2002, terrorists regularly made use of these centers because their rules were not as strict as onshore financial institutions. Accounts could be set up electronically using fictitious names or numbers. Money could be transferred electronically from one account to another with no questions asked. At the same time, OFCs guaranteed their customers' complete privacy. Anyone asking for information about an account was turned away.

Beginning around 1998, terrorists and other criminals learned that they had to be on guard, however, because U.S. government agencies, coupled with international organizations, began to demand greater disclosure from OFCs. Most OFCs agreed to cooperate. They changed their policies and began releasing information in order to help identify terrorists and other criminals. As of 2005, only five countries housing OFCs were not cooperative: Monaco, Andorra, Liberia, Liechtenstein, and the Marshall Islands. IRS commissioner Charles O. Rossotti stated: "The guarantee of secrecy associated with offshore banking is evaporating."[58] As a result, terrorists have had to give up OFCs almost entirely as hiding places for their funds.

Providing Freedom and Opportunity

In addition to countering terrorism with weapons, strong homeland defense, and improved financial intelligence, Western leaders tried to combat the problem by improving the political, social, and economic conditions in countries where people lack freedom and opportunity. They do this because they know that people who have a voice in government and hope for the future are less likely to embrace terrorism. As Vice President Dick Cheney observed in January 2004, "Terrorists do not find fertile recruiting grounds in societies where young people have the right to decide their own destinies and choose their own leaders."[59]

In Afghanistan, hard work helped improve social and economic conditions after the overthrow of the Taliban in 2002. The United States and other countries assisted in the establishment of a new democratic government. Aid helped build up the economy and provided options for farmers who had in the past raised opium poppies and been involved in the drug trade because it provided them the greatest income. Coalition troops and others helped maintain order so terrorism could not once again take root.

One tactic of the U.S. war on terror is fostering goodwill toward America among the general population of Afghanistan. This U.S. Army medic is treating an elderly Afghani man.

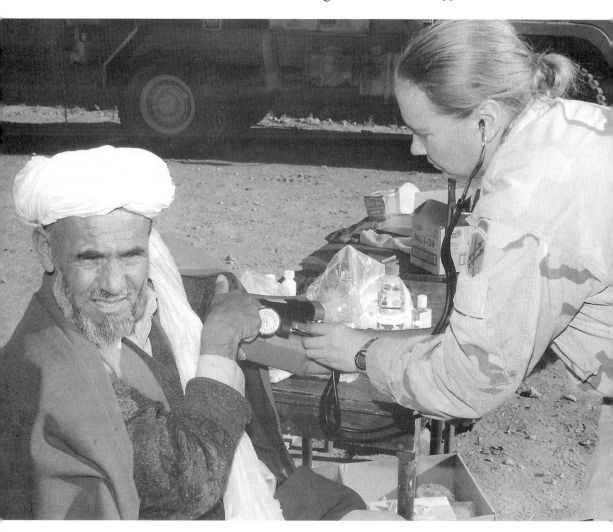

"We're investing in the development of Afghanistan to promote stability in this country and the wider region,"[60] Aly Mawji, a business developer, states. President Hamid Karzai concurs. "The international community should stay with Afghanistan if not for the interest of Afghanistan, then for their own interests,"[61] he says.

The Middle East—specifically Iraq—is another region where Western nations hope that improving social and economic conditions will quell terrorism. The Bush administration believes the establishment of a stable and democratic government, where all men and women can have a say in how they can live, worship, and earn a living, is the first step in ensuring that another tyrannical regime such as Saddam Hussein's does not gain control. As Bush stated in November 2003, "The failure of Iraqi democracy would embolden terrorists around the world, increase dangers to the American people, and extinguish the hopes of millions in the region."[62]

The United States and its allies also believe that the establishment of a stable, democratic, sovereign nation of Palestine will help deter terrorism in the Middle East. They believe that better conditions would go far to lessen the anger and frustration that many Palestinians feel, and will also give them hope for the future. All of that could lessen terrorism, too. As Bush noted in 2002, "A Palestinian state will never be created by terror—it will be built through reform. And reform must be more than cosmetic change, or veiled attempts to preserve the status quo. True reform will require entirely new political and economic institutions, based on democracy, market economics and action against terrorism."[63]

Controversy and Compromise

Countering terrorism by promoting freedom and democracy throughout the world is controversial to those who believe that democracy is not an appropriate fit for many countries, especially Muslim countries, whose citizens may prefer a government based on Islamic law. They point out that other types of governments, including authoritarian systems such as monarchies, can promote freedom and prosperity, too. On the other hand, if new democracies are weak, there is little to stop elected leaders from abusing their powers and transforming their offices into dictatorships. Correspondent Robert D. Kaplan says, "I submit that the democracy we are encouraging in many poor parts of the world is an integral [basic] part of a transformation towards new forms of authoritarianism [dictatorship]."[64]

Some people in the United States believe that their own government is already abusing its power, particularly after the passing of the Patriot Act. They see the act as a needless invasion of privacy and fear that it will be used to further erode constitutional and civil rights in the future. Other Americans, however, are comfortable with the act, pointing out that restrictions on civil liberties are sometimes necessary during times

Some critics of the USA Patriot Act believe that its antiterrorism provisions violate civil liberties.

of war. For instance, President Abraham Lincoln suspended the right of habeas corpus, a safeguard against unlawful imprisonment, during the Civil War. If steps such as those allowed by the act are not taken, they note, many innocent people could suffer at the hands of unrestricted terrorists. "The danger to our civil liberties comes from the terrorists . . . not the government's actions," said former U.S. attorney general William Barr. "I think the government's actions have been restrained, moderate, well within the law and pose no genuine civil liberties concerns."[65]

The issue of civil liberties versus national security promises to remain a hot topic as long as Americans work to fight terrorism. As the twenty-first century progresses, it is likely that they will have to continue to adjust and compromise, because terrorism itself will likely change as time passes. Forecasters Marvin J. Cetron and Owen Davies predict:

> In the past, terrorists have been ruthless opportunists, using a bloody, but relatively narrow, range of weapons to further clear, political ends. The [coming years] may well be the age of superterrorism, when they gain access to weapons of mass destruction and show a new willingness to use them. Tomorrow's most dangerous terrorists will be motivated not by political ideology, but by fierce ethnic and religious hatreds. Their goal will not be political control, but the utter destruction of their chosen enemies.[66]

6

Tomorrow's Terrorism

THE WORLD WILL have to face the issue of terrorism for many years to come. In societies marked by the rapid movement of people, goods, and services, and with easy access to information and new technologies, terrorists are increasingly able to operate on a global scale. The ease and affordability of worldwide travel means they do not have to carry out activities in a single region of the world. Connections to cellular phones, the Internet, and other types of electronic communication help them keep in touch, raise and exchange money, and plan their attacks from all points of the globe. "[Terrorists will become] an eclectic array of groups, cells and individuals that do not need a stationary headquarters,"[67] a 2005 report by the National Intelligence Council states.

Terrorists in the future may also become capable of using weapons of mass destruction, including biological, chemical, and nuclear material, developed solely for the purpose of terror. They may operate in cyberspace to destroy or manipulate computerized data for their own purposes. At the same time, they will continue to use conventional weapons in their attacks. Therefore, the war against terrorism must continually change to keep abreast of developing technology.

Biological and Chemical Terrorism

Chemical or biological agents are the likeliest weapons terrorists will use if they decide to stage a nonconventional attack in the future. Chemical agents range from cyanide and mustard gas to Sarin and VX (the deadliest nerve agent to date) and can kill or injure the people exposed to them almost immediately. They can be dispersed on a small scale when a container is opened and fumes escape, or on a larger scale, when released out of an airplane for instance. Saddam Hussein dropped bombs filled with mustard gas, nerve gas, and cyanide on Kurdish villagers in 1988, resulting in five thousand deaths. After that incident, bodies were found in the streets, where the victims had fallen just minutes after breathing in the deadly fumes.

Some nations have stockpiles of chemical agents that terrorists could access through theft, bribery, or some other means. They also have biological agents such as smallpox, anthrax, and bubonic plague, which are just as deadly as chemicals, but take time to develop in the human body. These agents can be passed through the air throughout the population during their incubation period (the time when a person is infectious but does not show symptoms). In the case of a biological attack by terrorists, large numbers of people would become sick, followed by more, until incidence rates reached epidemic proportions.

Trauma and Death

Biological agents can be "weaponized"—that is, processed to help them remain suspended in the air so that they spread farther and infect more people. They also have the potential to be genetically altered so that those people who are infected cannot be cured. If terrorists get their hands on something like weaponized anthrax, they could infect and kill an enormous number of people. Experts have estimated that if a large amount of weaponized anthrax particles were released under optimal weather conditions in a large city, 200,000 people in an area 40 miles (64.4km) downwind of the release would be infected. If untreated, 180,000 of them would die. If the anthrax had been altered to be antibiotic resistant, the death toll would be much higher. "[It is] one of the big things we're worried about," bioterrorism expert Philip K. Russel says. "Anthrax . . . can create a very big disaster."[68]

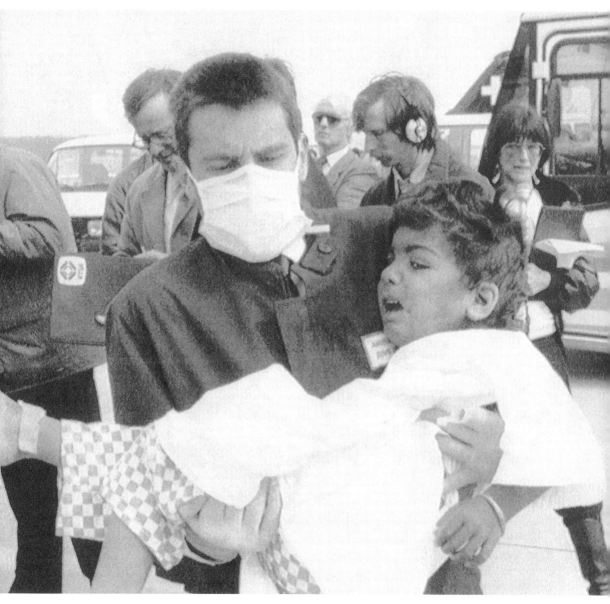

The world has already seen examples of the trauma and death produced by chemical and biological weapons. A 1995 Sarin gas attack on commuters in the Tokyo subway by the Japanese cult Aum Shinrikyo killed twelve people and sent more than five thousand others to hospitals. In the United States in October and November 2001, tiny amounts of weaponized anthrax were mailed to people on the East

Many Kurdish Iraqis, such as this young girl, suffered from nerve gas attacks launched by the government of deposed Iraqi president Saddam Hussein.

Terrorists released poisonous Sarin gas in a crowded Tokyo subway in 1995, exposing nearly six thousand people to the deadly nerve agent and killing twelve.

Coast, including newspeople at several television networks and several members of Congress. One man died of the disease, the FBI was called in to investigate, and millions of Americans worried every day when they opened their mail, fearing that deadly white powder would fall out. As of 2005 the perpetrator of the mailings has not been apprehended.

Although the terrorists in the latter case were never identified, some are more open in their efforts to obtain and use chemical and biological weapons. In 1998, Osama bin Laden publicly proclaimed that the acquisition of chemical or nuclear weapons should be the goal of every Islamic terrorist. In 2001 an al Qaeda operative tried to purchase anthrax for the terrorist network, but was unsuccessful. Al Qaeda spokesman Abu Gheith said in 2002, "It is our right to fight them [Americans] with chemical and biological weapons, so as to afflict them with fatal maladies that have afflicted the Muslims because of the [American] chemical and biological weapons."[69]

Nuclear Terrorism

Another type of terrorism that could pose a serious future threat is a nuclear attack. Al Qaeda leaders have already considered the possibility of carrying out a nuclear attack against the West, and the United States believes the Russian mafia, members of organized crime groups, provided the organization with some components needed for a nuclear bomb before 2001. "There are signs they [the Russian mafia] have been supplying [Bin Laden] with chemical and biological materials and nuclear components,"[70] said one U.S. official in 2001. The war in Afghanistan put their plans on hold. That does not mean, however, that at some future date they or some other terrorist group will not be ready to strike using a nuclear device of some kind.

There are others in addition to the Russian mafia who would be willing to provide nuclear weapons to terrorists. Weapons that were part of the former Soviet Union's biological weapons program are available for sale on the black market; nuclear weapons could be bought and sold in the same way. Former Soviet scientists who are out of work can be recruited for their nuclear expertise. Governments that sponsor terror are willing to provide support for terrorists, too. The Iranian government is vigorously pursuing programs to produce nuclear, chemical, and biological weapons. Syria is known to have a stockpile of the nerve agent Sarin and is trying to develop more toxic and persistent nerve agents.

The effects of a nuclear attack could be devastating. Even a relatively small ten-kiloton nuclear device, if exploded in a populated area, could kill half a million people and do $1 trillion in damage. The bomb would also release radiation—harmful energy—that would cover a wide region, causing sickness such as diarrhea, nausea, and even death within hours or days, and make the region too dangerous to live in for years to come.

A "dirty bomb" might kill fewer people but would still cause panic, and would spread toxic radioactive waste for large distance. A dirty bomb is a conventional bomb contaminated with low-level radioactive material such as that used at hospitals or factories. Terrorists find such material easier to access than a high-level nuclear device. A piece of radioactive cobalt from a food irradiation plant, for instance, if detonated in New York, could contaminate 380 square miles (611.5 sq km). Henry Kelly, president of the Federation of American Scientists, notes, "The entire borough of Manhattan would be so contaminated that anyone living there would have a 1 in 100 chance of dying from cancer caused by the . . . radiation. It would be decades before the city was inhabitable again, and demolition might be necessary."[71]

Cyberterrorism

While nuclear weapons are frightening, technology is also giving terrorists new means to hurt and intimidate those with whom they disagree. One of the most complex of these is cyberterrorism, where malicious software and electromagnetic and microwave weapons can be used to destroy data on computers and computer systems and cause massive disruption in the physical world.

Authorities fear that skilled hackers with terrorist intent will one day access, disable, or damage computer systems that control power or water supplies, gas and oil production, telecommunications or banking networks, and transportation or emergency services. The end result could be anything from a shutdown of Wall Street to the breaching of a dam, with tons of water flooding over residents living downstream. The potential for a disaster like this was illustrated in Russia in early 2000 when, with the help of a disgruntled employee, a group of hackers seized control of the computer systems of Gazprom, the largest oil and natural gas company in the country. Gazprom officials denied reports of the takeover, but one interior ministry spokesperson stated that

These firefighters are decontaminating the victim of a simulated radiological attack, one of many homeland security drills instituted since the September 11 attacks.

the flow of oil to much of the country was in the hackers' hands for several hours. Another senior official reported, "We were very close to a major natural disaster."[72]

In May 2003, FBI agents uncovered a budding cyberterrorist plot in the United States when they learned of hackers who sent an e-mail to the National Science Foundation (NSF), an independent federal agency with a focus on science, health, and national defense. In the e-mail, the hackers claimed to have penetrated the NSF network that controlled life-support systems for dozens of scientists at a South Pole research station. This was at a time when weather conditions would not permit aircraft to assist the station. The e-mail demanded money and "contained data only found on the NSF's computer systems, proving that this was no hoax,"[73] says Keith Lourdeau, deputy assistant director of the FBI's Cyber Division. The two hackers were quickly tracked down and arrested.

The FBI believes the cyberterrorist threat to the United States will expand in the future as terrorist groups hire or train hackers to help them add computer attacks to their more traditional approaches. Experts, note, however, that it is much easier for terrorists to use a bomb than it is to hack into a complex and protected computer system. In addition, explosives attract more attention on the evening news than does a cyberattack. Thus, cyberterror may never be the first weapon of choice for terrorists. As computer expert Laura Drake says, "[They want people to see] explosions and dismembered bodies on television rather than go after some unseen computer system, which isn't visible."[74]

Ecoterrorism

Ecoterrorists form another group that has demonstrated a potential for terror in the twenty-first century. Motivated to strike out against society in order to protect animals and the environment, these activists are loosely linked to a variety of organizations that include ALF and ELF, Pirates for Animal Liberation, Last Chance for Animals, and the Stop Huntingdon Animal Cruelty (SHAC). The latter is based in the United Kingdom, with cells in Germany, Italy, Portugal, and the United States.

Animal rights and environmental activists have existed since the 1970s. They have carried out attacks that include releasing animals from laboratories and fur farms, setting fire to car dealerships, and vandalizing new housing developments. Since 1976, groups such as ELF have committed more than eleven hundred criminal acts and caused property damage estimated at at least $110 million. A July 1998 fire on a ski resort in Vail, Colorado, caused $12 million in damage alone.

No human beings have been killed or injured in the attacks thus far, but in recent years, the movement has edged closer to such extreme violence. In 1999 eighty university researchers throughout the United States received threatening letters booby-trapped with razor blades. One of the letters, sent to a Harvard researcher, said, "You have until autumn 2000 to release all your primate [ape] captives and get out of the vivisection industry [the practice of injuring living animals for research]. If you do not heed our warning, your violence will be turned back upon you."[75] The "Justice Department" (an offshoot of ALF) claimed responsibility for the mailing.

In 2002, after ELF claimed responsibility for an arson attack on a U.S. Forest Service research facility in Irvine, Pennsylvania, causing more than $700,000 in damage, it issued a statement that express its willingness to take human life: "While innocent life will never be harmed in any action

Ecoterrorists set this auto dealership in West Covina, California, ablaze in August 2003 to protest the sale of gas-guzzling cars.

Some radical environmental groups oppose new housing developments. The Earth Liberation Front claimed responsibility for this fire that destroyed new homes in San Diego in August 2003.

we undertake, where it is necessary we will no longer hesitate to pick up the gun to implement justice."[76]

And in July 2004 animal rights activist Jerry Vlasak stated outright the direction he saw the movement taking in the future. Referring to scientists working in biomedical research, he said, "I think violence is part of the struggle against oppression. If something bad happens to these people, it will discourage others. It is inevitable that violence will be used in the struggle and that it will be effective."[77]

Ecoterrorism is becoming more common throughout the world in the twenty-first century, and authorities are paying greater attention to its adherents. Robert C. Rudge Jr., an FBI agent in Erie, Pennsylvania, noted in 2003, "Every FBI field office has had some situation involving ELF- and ALF-type activity. So it is a high priority for the bureau."[78]

Because terrorism—and the struggle against terrorism—will demand the world's attention for many years, patience will be a necessity in confronting the hostility of Islamic terrorists, domestic terrorists, cyberterrorists, and ecoterrorists. There will be victories and setbacks in the struggle. Mistakes will inevitably be made. Public policies will need adjustment. It may take years before counterterrorism measures show progress.

With patience, courage, and restraint, however, good ideas and wise political ideologies will lead to change for the better. And as more people understand the nature of terrorism, they will be better able to stand against it. As the U.S. government's 1997 Annual Defense Report notes, "Most important for any democracy in its struggle against terrorism is a public that is informed and engaged, and understands the nature of the threat. . . . It is how well the United States meets this challenge that will determine the winners, the losers, and the price paid by each."[79]

Notes

Introduction: What Is Terrorism?

1. United Nations Office on Drugs and Crime, "Definitions of Terrorism," 2005. www.unodc.org/unodc/terrorism_defi nitions. html.

2. The White House, "Remarks by the President to the Troops and Personnel," February 13, 2001. www.whitehouse.gov/ news/releases/20010213-1.html.

Chapter 1: The Scope of Terrorism

3. The White House "Address to a Joint Session of Congress and the American People," September 20, 2001. www. whitehouse.gov/news/releases/2001/09/20010920-8.html.

4. Carroll Payne, "Terrorist Motivation," *World Conflict Quarterly*, November 2000. www.globalterrorism101.com/ articleTerroristMotivation.html.

5. Fox News, "McVeigh's Apr. 26 Letter to Fox News," April 26, 2001. www.foxnews.com/story/0,2933,17500,00.html.

6. Paul G. Hawken, "A Report on the WTO/Seattle Conference," Global Vision, January 6, 2000. www.global-vision.org/worldviews/hawken1.html.

7. Thomas W. Lippman, "Inside the Mirage: America's Fragile Partnership with Saudi Arabia," Carnegie Council Books for Breakfast, June 2, 2004. www.carnegiecouncil.org/ viewMedia.php/prmTemplateID/8/prmID/4984.

8. Jim Garamone, "Bin Laden and the Al Qaeda Network," American Forces Information Service, February 14, 2002. www. au.af.mil/au/awc/awcgate/dod/n02142002_200202141.htm.

9. Quoted in *Observer*, "Full Text: Bin Laden's 'Letter to America,'" November 24, 2002. http://observer.guardian. co. uk/worldview/story/0,11581,845725,00.html.

10. Quoted in Federation of American Scientists Intelligence Resource Program, "The Covenant of the Hamas—Main Points," August 18, 1988. www.fas.org/irp/world/para/docs/880818a.htm.

11. Quoted in Reuters, "Chechen 'Terrorists' Part of Global Network: Putin," *Daily Times*, August 7, 2003. www.daily times.com.pk/default.asp?page=story_8-7-2003_pg4_3.

12. Liberation of Tigers Tamil Eelam, "V. Pirabakaran's Hero's Day Message—1999," November 27, 1999. www.tamil tigers.net/fallencomrades/martyrs_day_speech_1999.html.

13. Quoted in Martin McGuinness, "Bodenstown Speech," June 18, 1995. http://sinnfein.ie/peace/speech/12.

14. Bart Kosko, "Terror Threat May Be Mostly a Big Bluff: The Facts Point to Overestimation by a Frightened US," *Los Angeles Times*, September 13, 2004, p. B-11.

Chapter 2: The Logic and Tactics of Terrorism

15. Philip Ruddock, "Opening Address—The Private Business Public Interest: Collaborative Partnerships in the Quest for Security," Attorney General's Department (Australia), February 16, 2004. www.ag.gov.au/agd/WWW/MinisterRuddock Home.nsf/Page/Speeches_2004_Speeches_16_February_2004_-_Speech_to_Security_Quest_2004.

16. Terrorism Resource Center, "The Basics of Terrorism, Part 1: Terrorism Defined," May 20, 2000. www.isuisse.com/emmaf/base/baster.html.

17. Mike Pelletier, "Operation Backpack," *Desert Dispatch*, October 2004. www.nhmilitaryfamily.com/pdfs/nl_197bde_iraq_vol6.pdf.

18. Quoted in CNN.com, "Huge Madrid Rally Against ETA Talks," June 7, 2005. www.cnn.com/2005/WORLD/europe/06/04/spain.anti.eta.rally.ap/index.html.

19. Robert T. Thetford, "Terrorism: Target Selection and Symbolism," Institute for Criminal Justice Education, September 17, 2001. www.icje.org/id118.htm.

20. Quoted in Michael Moran, "Another 'Orange' for Fourth of July?" MSNBC, June 26, 2003. http://msnbc.msn.com/id/3070624.

21. Thomas Friedman, "Our Open Society Is in Danger in This New World War of Terror," *Sydney Morning Herald*, January 12, 2004. www.smh.com.au/articles/2004/01/11/1073769454367.html?from=storyrhs.

22. Ibrahim al-Marashi, "Iraq's Hostage Crisis: Kidnappings, Mass Media and the Iraqi Insurgency," *Middle East Review of International Affairs*, December 2004. http://meria.idc.ac.il/journal/2004/issue4/jv8no4a1.html.

23. Quoted in Jeff Jacoby, "Pearl Video Brings the Horror Home," *Boston Globe*, June 13, 2002, p. A-19.

24. Quoted in BBC News, "Hostages Speak of Storming Terror," October 26, 2002. http://news.bbc.co.uk/1/hi/world/europe/2363679.stm.

25. Council on Foreign Relations, "Terrorism and the Media," Terrorism: Questions & Answers, 2004. http://cfrterrorism.org/terrorism/media.html.

26. Quoted in Council on Foreign Relations, "Terrorism and the Media."

27. Rajat Madhok, "Are Terrorists Manipulating the World Media?" Philadelphia Independent Media Center, July 5, 2004. www.phillyimc.org/en/2004/07/13618.shtml.

28. Kevin LaGrandeur, "Terrorism on the Web," *Proceedings of the 2002 Conference of the Southwest Popular Culture Association*. www.geocities.com/klagrandeur/terrorpaper3.html.

Chapter 3: Terrorist Recruiting and Training

29. Matthew A. Levitt, "Hamas from Cradle to Grave," *Mid-

dle East Quarterly, Winter 2004. www.meforum.org/article/582.

30. Quoted in Levitt, "Hamas from Cradle to Grave."

31. Rohan Gunaratna, "Terror Unlimited," *Frontline*, September 29–October 12, 2001. www.hinduonnet.com/fline/fl1820/18200280.htm.

32. Quoted in Peter M. Forster, "The Psychology of Terror," Blue Oceans, 1999–2005. www.blue-oceans.com/psychology/terror_psych.html.

33. Forster, "The Psychology of Terror."

34. Quoted in Irwin J. Mansdorf, "The Psychological Framework of Suicide Terrorism," *Jerusalem Letter/Viewpoints*, April 15, 2003. www.jcpa.org/jl/vp496.htm.

35. Quoted in *USA Today*, "Israelis Stop Boy Wearing Bomb Vest," March 24, 2004. www.usatoday.com/news/world/2004-03-24-young-mideast-boy_X.htm.

36. Quoted in Nic Robertson, "Tapes Show Al Qaeda Trained for Urban Jihad on West," CNN.com, August 21, 2002. http://archives.cnn.com/2002/US/08/20/terror.tape.main/index.html.

37. Quoted in Robertson, "Tapes Show Al Qaeda Trained for Urban Jihad on West."

38. Arlene Kushner, "A Report on the UN Relief and Works Agency for Palestine Refugees in the Near East," Center for Near East Policy Research, March 2003. http://israelbehindthenews.com/Reports/UNWRAReport.pdf.

39. Quoted in Aish Hatorah, "Inside a Terrorist's Mind," August 4, 2002. www.aish.com/jewishissues/middleeast/Inside_a_Terrorists_Mind.asp.

Chapter 4: Financing Terrorism

40. Quoted in Mark Chediak, "Following the Money: Tracking Down Al Qaeda's Fund Raisers in Europe," *Frontline*,

January 25, 2005. www.pbs.org/wgbh/pages/frontline/ shows/front/special/finance.html.

41. Quoted in News24.com, "Al-Qaeda Still Finds Funding," August 24, 2004. www.news24.com/News24/World/ News/0,,2-10-1462_1577608,00.html.

42. Quoted in Michael Isikoff and Mark Hosenball, "Paying for Terror," *Newsweek*, May 12, 2004. www.msnbc.msn. com/id/4963025/site/newsweek.

43. Quoted in Mark Kelley, "Ex-NBA Great's Mosque Gave Money to Terrorist Fronts," *San Diego Union-Tribune*, February 10, 2005. www.signonsandiego.com/union trib/20050210/news_1n10mosque.html.

44. Quoted in U.S. Department of State, "President Announces Crackdown on Terrorist Financial Network," November 7, 2001. www.state.gov/s/ct/rls/rm/2001/5982. htm.

45. Quoted in Council on Foreign Relations, "Syria," Terrorism: Questions & Answers, 2004. http://cfrterrorism.org/ sponsors/syria.html.

46. Quoted in Government of Sri Lanka, "LTTE Stamp Flatly Refused by Canadian Authorities," August 25, 2000. www.priu.gov.lk/news_update/Current_Affairs/ ca200008/20000825LTTE_stamp_refused.htm.

47. Quoted in Sari Horwitz, "Cigarette Smuggling Linked to Terrorism," *Washington Post*, June 8, 2004. www.wash ingtonpost.com/wp-dyn/articles/A23384-2004Jun7.html.

48. Yael Shahar, "Tracing Bin Laden's Money: Easier Said than Done," International Policy Institute for Counter-Terrorism, September 21, 2001. www.ict.org.il/articles/ articledet.cfm?articleid=387.

49. Alvin James, "Prepared Statement at the Hearing on the Administration's National Money Laundering Strategy for 2001," U.S. Senate Committee on Banking, Housing, and Urban Affairs, September 26, 2001. http:// banking.senate.gov/01_09hrg/092601/james.htm.

50. Harjit Singh Sandhu and Patrick M. Jost, "The Hawala Alternative Remittance System and Its Role in Money Laundering," Interpol, January 2000. www.interpol.int/Public/FinancialCrime/MoneyLaundering/hawala/default. asp.

51. Quoted in Chediak, "Following the Money: Tracking Down Al Qaeda's Fund Raisers in Europe."

Chapter 5: Counterterrorism

52. The White House, "President Bush Releases National Strategy for Combating Terrorism," February 14, 2003. www.whitehouse.gov/news/releases/2003/02/20030214 7.html.

53. Quoted in John D. Banusiewicz, "New NATO Chem/Bio Battalion Starts Operations," American Forces Information Service, December 1, 2003. www.defenselink.mil/news/Dec2003/n12012003_200312011.html.

54. Amy Thomas, "Mission Detection: The Underwater Port Security System," Military.com, March 14, 2005. www.military.com/NewsContent/0,13319,uscgl_031405. 00.html.

55. Quoted in Kris Axtman, "The Terror Threat at Home, Often Overlooked," *Christian Science Monitor*," December 29, 2003. www.csmonitor.com/2003/1229/p02s01-usju. html.

56. Quoted in Rosa Yum, "FBI: Man Willing to Sell Bomb to al Qaida," WNEP.com, May 23, 2005. www.wnep.com/global/story.asp?s=3381875&ClientType=Printable.

57. Quoted in Dan Murphy, "Saudi Crackdown on Charities Seen as Incomplete," *Christian Science Monitor*, June 9, 2004. www.csmonitor.com/2004/0609/p07s02-wome. html.

58. Quoted in Barbara T. Kaplan and Patrick T. O'Brien, "Secrecy Associated with Offshore Banking Is Evaporating," Greenberg Traurig, April 2002. www.gtlaw. com/pub/alerts/2002/kaplanb_04.asp.

59. Quoted in Jim Garamone, "Cheney Says Democracies Must Confront Terror Together," American Forces Information Service, January 26, 2004. www.defenselink.mil/news/Jan2004/n01262004_200401262.html.

60. Quoted in Afghan News Network, "Karzai's Afghanistan, Poisoned by Heroin Habit, Seeks Investors," March 22, 2005. www.afghannews.net/index.php?action=show&type=news&id=2247.

61. Quoted in Afghan News Network, "Karzai's Afghanistan, Poisoned by Heroin Habit, Seeks Investors."

62. The White House, "President Bush Discusses Freedom in Iraq and the Middle East," November 6, 2003. www.whitehouse.gov/news/releases/2003/11/200311062.html.

63. The White House, "President Bush Calls for New Palestinian Leadership," June 24, 2002. www.whitehouse.gov/news/releases/2002/06/20020624-3.html.

64. Robert D. Kaplan, "Was Democracy Just a Moment?" *Atlantic Monthly*, December 1997. www.thirdworldtraveler.com/Democracy/DemocracyMoment_AM.html.

65. Quoted in Online NewsHour, "Liberty vs. Security," September 10, 2002. www.pbs.org/newshour/bb/terrorism/july-dec02/liberty_9-10.html.

66. Marvin J. Cetron with Owen Davies, "The Future Face of Terrorism," *Futurist*, November/December 1994. www.wfs.org/cetron94.htm.

Chapter 6: Tomorrow's Terrorism

67. Quoted in Dana Priest, "Iraq New Terror Breeding Ground," *Washington Post*, January 14, 2005. www.washingtonpost.com/wp-dyn/articles/A74602005Jan13.html.

68. Quoted in John Mintz, "Technical Hurdles Separate Terrorists from Biowarfare," *Washington Post*, December

30, 2004. http://healthandenergy.com/terrorists_and_bio
warfare.htm.

69. Abu Gheith, "Why We Fight America: Al-Qa'ida
Spokesman Explains September 11 and Declares Inten-
tions to Kill 4 Million Americans with Weapons of Mass
Destruction," Middle East Media Research Institute,
June 12, 2002. www.memri.org/bin/articles.cgi?Area=
egypt&ID=SP38802.

70. Quoted in Bill Gertz, "Bin Laden Terror Group Tries to
Acquire Chemical Arms," *Washington Times*, September
26, 2001, p. A3.

71. Henry Kelly, "Dirty Bombs: Response to a Threat," *FAS
Public Interest Report*, March/April 2002. www.fas.
org/faspir/2002/v55n2/dirtybomb.htm.

72. Quoted in Paul Quinn-Judge, "Cracks in the System,"
Time Europe, June 9, 2002. www.time.com/time/europe/
magazine/article/0,13005, 901020617260664,00. html.

73. Quoted in Dan Verton, "CIA to Issue Cyberterror Intelligence Estimate," Computerworld, February 24, 2004.
www.computerworld.com/printthis/2004/0,4814,90448,
00.html.

74. Quoted in James Gordon Meek, "Cyberterror: Thing
That Goes Bump in the Net?" Global Security.org., August 27, 1999. www.globalsecurity.org/intell/library/
news/1999/08/cyber0829_01.htm.

75. Quoted in Anti-Defamation League, "Ecoterrorism: Extremism in the Animal Rights and Environmentalist
Movements," 2005. www.adl.org/Learn/Ext_US/Eco
terrorism.asp.

76. Quoted in Anti-Defamation League, "Ecoterrorism."

77. Quoted in Anti-Defamation League, "Ecoterrorism."

78. Quoted in Ronald Ahrens, "Roar on Terrorism—Extended

Interviews," *Automobile*, June 2003. www.automobile mag. com/features/0306_Ahrens.

79. U.S. Department of Defense, "Responding to Terrorism," Annual Defense Report, 1997. www.defenselink.mil/ execsec/adr97/chap9.html#top.

Organizations to Contact

Central Intelligence Agency (CIA)
Office of Public Affairs
Washington, DC 20505
703-482-0623
www.cia.gov

The CIA calls itself the eyes and ears of America. Its Web site has a home page for kids, a variety of publications to send for or to download, employment opportunities for students and others at the agency, and much more.

Federal Bureau of Investigation (FBI)
J. Edgar Hoover Building
935 Pennsylvania Ave., NW
Washington, DC 20535-0001
202-324-3000
www.fbi.gov

The FBI fights domestic terrorism, cyberterrorism, as well as conventional crime. Its Web site gives information on counterterrorism efforts, plus offers a variety of reports and publications, a list of most wanted terrorists, and procedures for submitting a tip.

Financial Action Task Force (FATF)
2, rue André Pascal
75775 Paris Cedex 16
France
contact@fatf-gafi.org
www.fatf-gafi.org

The FATF focuses on spreading the anti–money laundering

message to all continents and regions of the globe, monitoring the implementation of the recommendations they established among their members, and reviewing money laundering trends and countermeasures. The Web site contains publications, news and events, resources and links, and an annual report.

Terrorism Research Center (TRC)
877-635-0816
TRC@terrorism.com
www.terrorism.com/index.php

Founded in 1996, the Terrorism Research Center is an independent institute dedicated to the research of terrorism, information warfare and security, critical infrastructure protection, homeland security, and other issues of low-intensity political violence. The Web site includes answers to frequently asked questions, terrorist and terrorist group profiles, significant terror events, and more.

U.S. Department of Homeland Security (DHS)
Washington, DC 20528
202-282-8000
www.dhs.gov/dhspublic

The DHS has as its mission to lead the unified national effort to secure America. It works to prevent and deter terrorist attacks and protect against and respond to threats and hazards to the nation. It tries to ensure safe and secure borders, welcome lawful immigrants and visitors, and promote the free flow of commerce. Its Web site provides information on the various components of the department.

For Further Reading

Books

Kathlyn Gay, *Silent Death: The Threat of Chemical and Biological Terrorism*. Brookfield, CT: Twenty-First Century Books, 2001. This book discusses various biological and chemical agents, their use throughout history, and the possibility of their use by terrorists in the future.

Ted Gottfried, *Homeland Security Versus Constitutional Rights*. Brookfield, CT: Twenty-First Century Books, 2003. The author examines both sides of the question: Are we defending our nation against terrorism at the expense of the rights of the individual citizen?

Samuel M. Katz, *Jihad: Islamic Fundamentalist Terrorism*. Minneapolis: Lerner, 2004. This book covers the history of Islam and fundamentalism, Egypt's jihad warriors, Lebanon's Hizballah, and al Qaeda's international network.

Milton Meltzer, *The Day the Sky Fell: A History of Terrorism*. New York: Random House, 2002. The author shows that terrorism is as old as humankind and has been the tool of many groups throughout history.

Works Consulted

Periodicals

Bill Gertz, "Bin Laden Terror Group Tries to Acquire Chemical Arms," *Washington Times*, September 26, 2001, p. A3.

Jeff Jacoby, "Pearl Video Brings the Horror Home," *Boston Globe*, June 13, 2002.

Bart Kosko, "Terror Threat May Be Mostly a Big Bluff: The Facts Point to Overestimation by a Frightened US," *Los Angeles Times*, September 13, 2004.

Internet Sources

Afghan News Network, "Karzai's Afghanistan, Poisoned by Heroin Habit, Seeks Investors," March 22, 2005. www. afghannews.net/index.php?action=show&type=news&id= 2247.

Ronald Ahrens, "Roar on Terrorism—Extended Interviews," *Automobile*, June 2003. www.automobilemag.com/features/ 0306-Ahrens.

Aish HaTorah, "Inside a Terrorist's Mind," August 4, 2002. www.aish.com/jewishissues/middleeast/Inside_a_Terrorists _Mind.asp.

Anti-Defamation League, "Ecoterrorism: Extremism in the Animal Rights and Environmentalist Movements," 2005. www.adl.org/Learn/Ext_US/Ecoterrorism.asp.

Kris Axtman, "The Terror Threat at Home, Often Overlooked," *Christian Science Monitor*," December 29, 2003. www. csmonitor.com/2003/1229/p02s01-usju.html.

John D. Banusiewicz, "New NATO Chem/Bio Battalion Starts Operations," American Forces Information Service, December 1, 2003. www.defenselink.mil/news/Dec2003/n12012003_200312011.html.

BBC News, "Hostages Speak of Storming Terror," October 26, 2002. http://news.bbc.co.uk/1/hi/world/europe/ 2363 679.stm.

Marvin J. Cetron with Owen Davies, "The Future Face of Terrorism," Futurist, November/December 1994. www.wfs.org/cetron94.htm.

Mark Chediak, "Following the Money: Tracking Down Al Qaeda's Fund Raisers in Europe," Frontline, January 25, 2005. www.pbs.org/wgbh/pages/frontline/shows/front/special/finance.html.

Council on Foreign Relations, "Syria," Terrorism Questions & Answers, 2004. http://cfrterrorism.org/sponsors/syria.html.

———, "Terrorism and the Media," Terrorism: Questions & Answers, 2004. http://cfrterrorism.org/terrorism/media.html.

Federation of American Scientists Intelligence Resource Program, "The Covenant of the Hamas—Main Points," August 18, 1988. www.fas.org/irp/world/para/docs/880818a.htm.

Peter M. Forster, "The Psychology of Terror," Blue Oceans, 1999–2005. www.blue-oceans.com/psychology/terror_psych.html.

Fox News, "McVeigh's Apr. 26 Letter to Fox News," April 26, 2001. www.foxnews.com/story/0,2933,17500,00.html.

Thomas Friedman, "Our Open Society Is in Danger in This New World War of Terror," Sydney Morning Herald, January 12, 2004. www.smh.com.au/articles/2004/01/11/10 73769454367.html?from=storyrhs.

Daya Gamage, "LTTE Still Has 1,250 Child Soldiers—The Latest Global Report Says," Asian Tribune, November 20, 2004. www.asiantribune.com/show_news.php?id= 12168.

Jim Garamone, "Bin Laden and the Al Qaeda Network," American Forces Information Service, February 14, 2002. www.au.af.mil/au/awc/awcgate/dod/n02142002_2002021 41.htm.

———, "Cheney Says Democracies Must Confront Terror Together," American Forces Information Service, January 26, 2004. www.defenselink.mil/news/Jan2004/n01262004 _200401262.html.

Abu Gheith, "Why We Fight America: Al-Qa'ida Spokes-man Explains September 11 and Declares Intentions to Kill 4 Million Americans with Weapons of Mass Destruc-tion," June 12, 2002. www.memri.org/bin/articles.cgi? Area=egypt&ID=SP38802.

Government of Sri Lanka, "LTTE Stamp Flatly Refused by Canadian Authorities," August 25, 2000. www.priu. gov.1k/news_update/Current_Affairs/ca200008/2000082 5LTTE_stamp_refused.htm.

Rohan Gunaratna, "Terror Unlimited," *Frontline*, September 29–October 12, 2001. www.hinduonnet.com/fline/fl1820/ 18200280.htm.

Paul G. Hawken, "A Report on the WTO/Seattle Confer-ence," Global Vision, January 6, 2000. www.globalvision. org/worldviews/hawken1.html.

Sari Horwitz, "Cigarette Smuggling Linked to Terrorism," *Washington Post*, June 8, 2004. www.washingtonpost. com/wp-dyn/articles/A23384-2004Jun7.html.

Michael Isikoff and Mark Hosenball, "Paying for Terror," *Newsweek*, May 12, 2004. www.msnbc.msn.com/id/ 4963025/site/newsweek.

Alvin James, "Prepared Statement at the Hearing on the Ad-ministration's National Money Laundering Strategy for 2001," U.S. Senate Committee on Banking, Housing, and Urban Affairs, September 26, 2001. http://banking.senate. gov/01_09hrg/092601/james.htm.

Barbara T. Kaplan and Patrick T. O'Brien, "Secrecy Associated with Offshore Banking Is Evaporating," Greenberg Traurig, April 2002. www.gtlaw.com/pub/alerts/2002/kaplanb_04.asp.

Robert D. Kaplan, "Was Democracy Just a Moment?" *Atlantic Monthly*, December 1997. www.thirdworldtraveler.com/Democracy/DemocracyMoment_AM.html.

Mark Kelley, "Ex-NBA Great's Mosque Gave Money to Terrorist Fronts," *San Diego Union-Tribune*, February 10, 2005. www.signonsandiego.com/uniontrib/20050210/news_1n10mosque.html.

Henry Kelly, "Dirty Bombs: Response to a Threat," *FAS Public Interest Report*, March/April 2002. www.fas.org/faspir/2002/v55n2/dirtybomb.htm.

Keralanext.com, "Huge Madrid Rally Against ETA Talks," June 7, 2005. www.Keralanext.com/news/readnext,l.asp?id=221681&pg=2.

Arlene Kushner, "A Report on the UN Relief and Works Agency for Palestine Refugees in the Near East," Center for Near East Policy Research, March 2003. http://israelbehindthenews.com/Reports/UNWRAReport.pdf.

Kevin LaGrandeur, "Terrorism on the Web," *Proceedings of the 2002 Conference of the Southwest Popular Culture Association*. www.geocities.com/klagrandeur/terrorpaper3.html.

Matthew A. Levitt, "Hamas from Cradle to Grave," *Middle East Quarterly*, Winter 2004. www.meforum.org/article/582.

Liberation Tigers of Tamil Eelam, "V. Pirabakaran's Hero's Day Message—1999," November 27, 1999. www.tamiltigers.net/fallencomrades/martyrs_day_speech_1999.html.

Thomas W. Lippman, "Inside the Mirage: America's Fragile Partnership with Saudi Arabia," Carnegie Council Books for Breakfast, June 2, 2004. www.carnegiecouncil.org/viewMedia.php/prmTemplateID/8/prmID/4984.

Rajat Madhok, "Are Terrorists Manipulating the World Media?" Philadelphia Independent Media Center, July 5, 2004. www.phillyimc.org/en/2004/07/13618.shtml.

Irwin J. Mansdorf, "The Psychological Framework of Suicide Terrorism," *Jerusalem Letter/Viewpoint*, April 15, 2003. www.jcpa.org/jl/vp496.htm.

Ibrahim al-Marashi, "Iraq's Hostage Crisis: Kidnappings, Mass Media and the Iraqi Insurgency," *Middle East Review of International Affairs*, December 2004. http://meria.idc.ac. il/journal/2004/issue4/jv8no4al.html.

Martin McGuinness, "Bodenstown Speech," June 18, 1995. http://sinnfein.ie/peace/speech/12.

James Gordon Meek, "Cyberterror: Thing That Goes Bump in the Net?" Global Security.org., August 27, 1999. www.globalsecurity.org/intell/library/news/1999/08/cyber 0829_01.htm.

John Mintz, "Technical Hurdles Separate Terrorists from Biowarfare," *Washington Post*, December 30, 2004. http://heal thandenergy.com/terrorists_and_biowarfare.htm.

Michael Moran, "Another 'Orange' for Fourth of July?" MSNBC, June 26, 2003. http://msnbc.msn.com/id/3070 624.

Dan Murphy, "Saudi Crackdown on Charities Seen as Incomplete," *Christian Science Monitor*, June 9, 2004. www.csmonitor.com/2004/0609/p07s02-wome.html.

News24.com, "Al-Qaeda Still Finds Funding," August 24, 2004. www.news24.com/News24/World/News/0,,2-10-14 62_1577608,00.html.

Observer, "Full Text: Bin Laden's 'Letter to America,'" November 24, 2002. http://observer.guardian.co.uk/world-view/story/0,11581,845725,00.html.

Online NewsHour, "Liberty vs. Security," September 10, 2002. www.pbs.org/newshour/bb/terrorism/july-dec02/liberty_9-10.html.

Carroll Payne, "Terrorist Motivation," *World Conflict Quarterly*, November 2000. www.globalterrorism101.com/articleTerroristMotivation.html.

Mike Pelletier, "Operation Backpack," *Desert Dispatch*, October 2004. www.nhmilitaryfamily.com/pdfs/nl_197bde_iraq_vol6.pdf.

Dana Priest, "Iraq New Terror Breeding Ground," *Washington Post*, January 14, 2005. www.washingtonpost.com/wp-dyn/articles/A7460-2005Jan13.html.

Paul Quinn-Judge, "Cracks in the System," *Time Europe*, June 9, 2002. www.time.com/time/europe/magazine/article/0,13005,901020617-260664,00.html.

Reuters, "Chechen 'Terrorists' Part of Global Network: Putin," *Daily Times*, August 7, 2003. www.dailytimes.com.pk/default.asp?page=story_8-7-2003_pg4_3.

Nic Robertson, "Tapes Show Al Qaeda Trained for Urban Jihad on West," CNN.com, August 21, 2002. http://archives.cnn.com/2002/US/08/20/terror.tape.main/index.html.

Philip Ruddock, "Opening Address—The Private Business Public Interest: Collaborative Partnerships in the Quest for Security," Attorney General's Department (Australia), February 16, 2004. www.ag.gov.au/agd/WWW/Minister RuddockHome.nsf/Page/Speeches_2004_Speeches_16_February_2004_-_Speech_to_Security_Quest_2004.

Harjit Singh Sandhu and Patrick M. Jost, "The Hawala Alternative Remittance System and Its Role in Money Laundering," Interpol, January 2000. www.interpol.int/Public/FinancialCrime/MoneyLaundering/hawala/default.asp.

Yael Shahar, "Tracing Bin Laden's Money: Easier Said than Done," International Policy Institute for Counter-Terrorism, September 21, 2001. www.ict.org.il/articles/articledet.cfm?articleid=387.

Terrorism Resource Center, "The Basics of Terrorism, Part 1:

Terrorism Defined," May 20, 2000. www.isuisse.com/emmaf/base/baster.html.

Robert T. Thetford, "Terrorism: Target Selection and Symbolism," Institute for Criminal Justice Education, September 17, 2001. http://www.icje.org/id118.htm.

Amy Thomas, "Mission Detection: The Underwater Port Security System," Military.com, March 14, 2005. www.military.com/NewsContent/0,13319,uscg1_031405.00.html.

United Nations Office on Drugs and Crime, "Definitions of Terrorism," 2005. www.unodc.org/unodc/terrorism_defi nitions.html.

USA Today, "Israelis Stop Boy Wearing Bomb Vest," March 24, 2004. www.usatoday.com/news/world/2004-03-24-young-mideast-boy_x.htm.

U.S. Department of Defense, "Responding to Terrorism," Annual Defense Report, 1997. www.defenselink.mil/execsec/adr97/chap9.html#top.

U.S. Department of State, "President Announces Crackdown on Terrorist Financial Network," November 7, 2001. www.state.gov/s/ct/rls/rm/2001/5982.htm.

Dan Verton, "CIA to Issue Cyberterror Intelligence Estimate," Computerworld, February 24, 2004. www.com puterworld.com/printthis/2004/0,4814,90448,00.html.

The White House "Address to a Joint Session of Congress and the American People," September 20, 2001. www.whitehouse.gov/news/releases/2001/09/20010920-8.html.

——, "President Bush Calls for New Palestinian Leadership," June 24, 2002. www.whitehouse.gov/news/releases/2002/06/20020624-3.html.

——, "President Bush Discusses Freedom in Iraq and the Middle East," November 6, 2003. www.whitehouse.gov/news/releases/2003/11/20031106-2.html.

————, "President Bush Releases National Strategy for Combatting Terrorism," February 14, 2003. www.white house.gov/news/releases/2003/02/20030214-7.html.

————, "Remarks by the President to the Troops and Personnel," February 13, 2001. www.whitehouse.gov/news/releases/20010213-1.html.

Rosa Yum, "FBI: Man Willing to Sell Bomb to al Qaida," WNEP.com, May 23, 2005. www.wnep.com/global/story.asp?s=3381875&ClientType=Printable.

Index

Picture Credits

About the Author

Diane Yancey lives in the Pacific Northwest with her husband, Michael; their dog, Gelato; and their cats, Newton and Lily. She has written more than twenty-five books for middle-grade and high school readers, including *Life of an American Soldier in Afghanistan*, *Leaders and Generals*, and *The Homefront: The War in Iraq*.